Let Us Keep The Feast

in Historic Beaufort

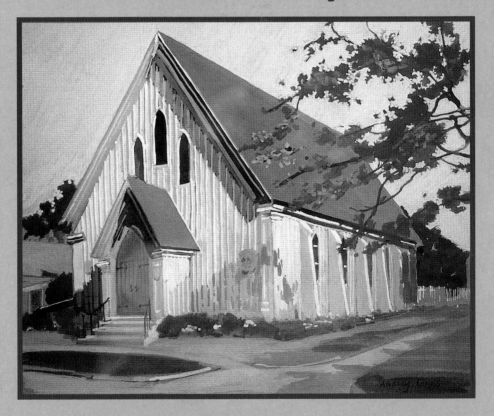

St. Paul's Episcopal Church Women
Beaufort, North Carolina

We see St. Paul's Episcopal Church, Beaufort, as the spiritual center of our community through loving, caring, and sharing: a parish that exemplifies the fellowship of Christ within the tradition of the Anglican community - a link to the past and a guide to the future. The Episcopal Church Women nurture our parish, community, and world through our outreach programs and provide fellowship for all parish women as we work together to further the mission of Christ's call.

Library of Congress Control Number: 20011087194
ISBN Number: 0-9708680-0-6

For additional copies, contact:
St. Paul's Episcopal Church
215 Ann Street
Beaufort, North Carolina 28516
252-728-3324

WIMMER
C O O K B O O K S
ConsolidatedGraphics

1-800-548-2537

Introduction

Let Us Keep the Feast in Historic Beaufort has been lovingly compiled and published by the Episcopal Church Women of St. Paul's Episcopal Church in Beaufort, North Carolina.

St. Paul's is the second oldest Episcopal Church in the state. It, like Beaufort, has a colorful history, beginning almost as early as the town itself. Soon after Beaufort began to be settled in 1709, an Act of Establishment was passed declaring that all laws in force in England for the establishment of the Church were to be in effect in North Carolina. By 1715, a new vestry act passed, dividing North Carolina into regional parishes. Beaufort was a part of Craven parish. Then in 1723, one year after Beaufort's official incorporation as a town, Carteret precinct was designated as St. John's parish.

Over the next fifty years, services were held several times a year throughout the county since there was no proper church building or permanent rector. Then in 1774, a Beaufort resident left a sum of money for the construction of a church. However, in 1776, as construction was almost complete, the Revolutionary War would cause the Church of England to disappear from Beaufort.

A period of inactivity followed until shortly before the Civil War. In September of 1855, a new parish was organized and named St. Paul's. A year later, land was purchased for ten dollars where the present church would be built. The cornerstone was laid in 1857 and the building was consecrated in 1861. The current pews are the original "temporary" pews.

But war would once again prove disastrous to the parish. The first St. Paul's School, opened in 1858, was closed in 1867. The church building remained intact, but the congregation was inactive. However, in 1899, under the guidance of Mrs. Nannie Geffroy and the Rev. Thomas P. Noe, St. Paul's School reopened, indicating the church was resurging as well. The school operated until 1939. In 1951, a rectory was built on the site. It is now the church office. The parish house is on the site of the old dormitory and dining hall.

During the past century, there has been continuous growth and change. Currently, there are 500 members who contribute vigorously to the life and mission of this active parish. However, the historical plaque on the church front - Est. 1857 - is a constant reminder of the long and significant existence of St. Paul's Episcopal Church and its contributions to our community and Diocese.

Alleluia. Christ our Passover is sacrificed for us.
Therefore, **Let us Keep the Feast**. *Alleluia.*
From the Holy Eucharist I and II

Summarized from **A Brief History of St. Paul's Church**
by the Rev'd. Matthew Stockard, Rector 1989-1999.

Historic Beaufort

Nearly 300 years ago, in 1709, a group of English and French Huguenots landed on the site of a former Indian village called Fish Town, seeking to establish a deep water port. The name of the town was later changed to Beaufort, honoring Henry Somerset, Duke of Beaufort, a descendant of one of the original Lord's Proprietors. Beaufort is the third oldest town in North Carolina, becoming incorporated in 1722.

Located on the middle coast of North Carolina and beautifully situated on Taylor's Creek near Atlantic Beach, Cape Lookout, and the Inland Waterway, Beaufort offers history, beauty, coastal waters, fishing, boating, and wonderful seafood. The town has survived invasions by pirates, the Spanish and British, two wars, and several major hurricanes. It is amazing, therefore, that the plan of Beaufort laid out in 1713 still exists in a twelve block area which is on the National Register of Historic Places. The original street names remain, honoring English royalty - Moore, Craven, Ann, Orange, Queen, and Pollock.

As is still common today, things moved slowly in the early days. In the later half of the 1700's, a canal finally joined the town and inland areas, opening up new business opportunities. More people began arriving, bringing new construction of homes as well as businesses. Some of these same houses remain today and have been restored either as private homes or as part of the Beaufort Historic Site.

Many of the same families that helped establish Beaufort continue to live here today through their descendants. Names like Bell, Ward, Whitehurst, Moore, Fulford, Potter, Ramsey, Johnson, Thomas, Duncan, Dickinson, Lewis, and Davis are still common.

In the past fifteen years there has been another growth spurt mainly due to the arrival of those who have discovered the slow and easy life in the charming town of Beaufort. In many ways, "Beaufort is today as it was yesterday - the same streets, the same feeling, the same pace, only with the modern changes that 300 years of science and technology can bring."

Adapted from *Beaufort- Yesterday and Today*
by Mamré Marsh Wilson

The 200 block of Ann Street as it appeared in 1900

L to R - Davis House, St. Paul's School Dormitory,
St. Paul's Episcopal Church, St. Paul's School, Arendell House

2

Table of Contents

Cover Artwork

Beaufort Waterfront - Watercolor

Nancy L. Rogers

Nancy L. Rogers, A.S.I.D. is our cover artist. A native of Salisbury, N.C., she lived in New Bern, N.C. for many years and would often come to Beaufort to paint. She began her study of art as a child, graduated from Duke University, and continued studies at Columbia and New York University. She has studied further in both the United States and Europe. She is a member of numerous art leagues and societies and has been juried in shows in several states. Mrs. Rogers serves on the Membership Board of the N.C. Museum of Art. She was featured in a show with four other artists at the Maritime Museum in Beaufort in the fall of 2000.

Title Page Artwork

St. Paul's Episcopal Church - Gouache Medium

Audrey Evans

Mrs. Evans of Cornwall, England, is a long-time friend of fellow artist Millie Voorhees and the late Ed Voorhees of Morehead City. She has been to the Beaufort and Morehead City area often to visit them and to paint. She studied art in England where she teaches and owns an art school with her husband.

Appetizers and Beverages

Still Life - Watercolor

Jim Williams

Mr. Williams, a retired patent attorney, is a member of St. Paul's.
He began art lessons at Carteret Community College soon after
moving to Beaufort in the early 1990's. He works mainly in
watercolors and enjoys nautical themes as subjects.

Mary Sterling's Crab Spread

1	shallot, chopped	6-8	ounces seafood cocktail sauce
1	tablespoon Worcestershire sauce	8	ounces lump crabmeat
1	(8-ounce) package cream cheese, softened		Fresh parsley, chopped

- Mix shallot and Worcestershire sauce into cream cheese.
- Spread mixture on a round tray or platter.
- Pour cocktail sauce on top.
- Add crabmeat to cover cheese.
- Sprinkle with chopped parsley to garnish.
- Chill and serve with crackers.

Yield: 8 servings

Front Street Shrimp Spread

3	pounds fresh shrimp, peeled and deveined	½	cup real mayonnaise
¼-½	cup butter		Worcestershire sauce, garlic salt and lemon juice to taste
2	(8-ounce) packages cream cheese, softened		

- Cook shrimp in butter, in small amounts, until done.
- Set aside, reserve liquid.
- Cream the cheese with mayonnaise and seasonings.
- Cut shrimp into bite-size pieces.
- Blend shrimp, cheese mixture and reserved liquid to a good dipping or spreading consistency.

Yield: 16 servings

Serve with crusty bread or crackers.

Clam Crisps

1 tablespoon butter	1 teaspoon Worcestershire sauce
2 tablespoons finely chopped onion	Dash garlic powder
1½ tablespoons flour	14 slices white bread, crusts removed and rolled very thin
1 (6½-ounce) can minced clams with liquid	½ cup butter, melted

- Cook onion in butter.
- Blend in flour, then clams and liquid.
- Add Worcestershire sauce and garlic powder, cool.
- Spread on bread.
- Roll up in jellyroll fashion and roll in melted butter.
- Cut each roll into 4 pieces.
- Place on a baking sheet and place in preheated 450° oven for about 10 minutes.

Yield: 56 Crisps

Can be made ahead and frozen; remove about 15 to 20 minutes before ready to bake.

Seviche

1	pound fresh fish	1	small can chopped mushrooms
1	cup chopped celery	1	small tomato, chopped
1	cup green olives	2	jalapeño peppers, chopped
½	cup chopped onions	½	teaspoon lemon pepper
	Garlic juice		marinade
1	tablespoon olive oil		Freshly squeezed lime juice

- Cut fish into very small pieces.
- Place in large container with airtight lid and add all other ingredients except lime juice.
- Cover this with enough lime juice to just cover, too much juice can make it sour.
- Cover with airtight lid and refrigerate 24 to 36 hours.
- Stir several times while marinating.
- Drain and serve cold on platter with crackers.

Yield: 5 to 6 cups

Will keep one week if refrigerated.

"Stillwater Café"
Black-Eyed Pea Cakes

4 cups dried black-eyed peas, rinsed in cold water	1 cup minced green onion
	Juice of 1 lime
12 cups water	2 cups diced tomato
2 teaspoons salt	1 teaspoon cumin
1 cup diced red pepper	1 teaspoon thyme
½ cup diced green pepper	1 teaspoon white pepper
5 tablespoons minced cilantro	1 teaspoon garlic powder
1 cup minced red onion	Bread crumbs
½ packet sugar substitute	2 ounces butter
2 cups fresh bread crumbs	2 ounces olive oil

- Combine peas, water and salt in heavy saucepan.
- Bring to a boil.
- Reduce to a simmer and cook until peas are very soft - about 1 hour.
- Place peas in a colander to drain and cool.
- Toss peas with all other ingredients except butter and olive oil and mix well.
- Form mixture into round cakes - about 2 ounces each.
- Dust with extra bread crumbs.
- Sauté cakes in skillet over medium to high heat using butter and olive oil.
- Cook about 2 to 3 minutes on each side.
- Drain on paper towels.

Yield: 48 cakes

Spinach-Stuffed Pasta Shells

1	(12-ounce) box large pasta shells	1	medium onion, diced
2	(10-ounce) packages frozen chopped spinach	1	(6-ounce) can water chestnuts, diced
1½	cups sour cream	½	cup Parmesan cheese
1½	cups mayonnaise	2	teaspoons dill weed
2	packages dry vegetable soup or dip mix	½	teaspoon salt
		¼	teaspoon pepper

- Cook pasta according to directions.
- Drain well and cool.
- Cook spinach according to microwave directions.
- Drain well.
- Mix spinach with all the other ingredients.
- Fill each shell with stuffing - approximately 1 tablespoon per shell.
- Chill thoroughly before serving.

Yield: 2 dozen

Stuffing also works well as a spread for vegetables or crackers.

Zucchini Appetizers

3	cups thinly sliced zucchini, unpared	½	teaspoon seasoned salt
1	cup biscuit mix	½	teaspoon dried oregano or marjoram
½	cup finely chopped onion		Dash pepper
½	cup grated Parmesan cheese	1	clove garlic, minced
2	tablespoons snipped parsley	½	cup oil
½	teaspoon salt	4	eggs, beaten

- Preheat oven to 350°.
- Grease 9 x 13-inch baking pan.
- Mix all ingredients together and spread in pan.
- Bake for 30 minutes or until golden brown.
- Cut into 2 x 2-inch pieces to serve.

Yield: 48 pieces

Martha's Stuffed Mushrooms

12	ounces fresh mushrooms	2	cups fresh bread crumbs
3	tablespoons margarine	¼	cup Parmesan cheese
½	medium onion, finely chopped	¾	cup chicken broth
½	green pepper, finely chopped		Salt and pepper to taste
½	teaspoon dried thyme		

- Cut stems from mushrooms and clean out cavity. Chop stems.
- Melt margarine in skillet. Sauté stems, onion and green pepper in margarine until tender.
- Add thyme and bread crumbs and blend. Add cheese, then broth until mixture is moist.
- Stuff caps with mixture. Place on greased baking sheet.
- Bake at 375° for about 20 minutes or until browned. Serve hot.

Yield: approximately 16 mushrooms

Veggie Bars

2	(8-ounce) cans crescent rolls	½	cup chopped fresh broccoli
2	(8-ounce) packages cream cheese, softened	¼	cup sliced black olives
½	cup mayonnaise	½	cup chopped yellow or red pepper
1	(1-ounce) packet ranch dressing seasoning	1	cup shredded sharp Cheddar cheese
½	cup sliced fresh mushrooms		

- Spread rolls out in a jellyroll pan. Press seams together.
- Bake at 400° for 10 minutes, cool.
- Mix cream cheese, mayonnaise and seasoning. Spread over crust.
- Mix vegetables together and sprinkle over above mixture.
- Top with cheese. Refrigerate.
- Slice into bars and serve.

Yield: 36 to 48 bars

Vegetable Spread

1	cucumber	¼	cup water
1	onion	2	cups mayonnaise
1	tomato, seeded		Salt and pepper to taste
1	green pepper	1	tablespoon Worcestershire sauce
1	pack plain gelatin		

- Dice vegetables into small pieces.
- Dissolve gelatin in water and slowly add to mayonnaise.
- Add to vegetables and mix well.
- Add salt, pepper and Worcestershire and stir.
- Refrigerate several hours before serving.
- Serve with crackers.

Yield: 4 cups

Mushroom Pâté

2 tablespoons butter	2-3 tablespoons sherry or Madeira wine
8 ounces fresh mushrooms, finely chopped	4 ounces softened cream cheese
1½ teaspoons minced fresh garlic	2 tablespoons butter
¼ cup minced green onions (white only)	2 tablespoons chopped parsley or green onion tops
⅓ cup chicken broth	

- Heat 2 tablespoons of butter in a skillet, add mushrooms and garlic and sauté 2 to 3 minutes.

- Add onion and sauté 1 minute more.

- Add chicken broth and cook until liquid evaporates.

- Add sherry and mix in cream cheese, butter and parsley.

- Cool to room temperature.

- Put in crock or bowl - keep refrigerated.

Yield: 8 to 10 servings

Serve with crackers or rye rounds.

Veggie Mousse

2	carrots, peeled	1	small tomato, peeled
2	teaspoons grated onion	1	package plain gelatin
2	medium cucumbers, peeled and	1	cup mayonnaise
	seeded	1	teaspoon salt
1	green pepper, chopped	1½	teaspoons sugar
1	stalk celery, chopped		Dash pepper

- Grate carrots and onion in food processor. Remove to large mixing bowl.

- Chop cucumber, green pepper, celery and tomato. Add to carrots and onion.

- Drain all vegetables in a colander and reserve juices. Return to mixing bowl.

- Sprinkle gelatin in 3 tablespoons of reserved liquids. Heat over low heat until dissolved.

- Add mayonnaise and seasonings and mix well. Add vegetables and mix well.

- Place in 4-cup mold and refrigerate until firm.

- Serve with crackers.

Yield: 4 cups

Pesto Loaf

½ cup oil packed sun-dried   1 pound thinly sliced provolone
   tomatoes   cheese

Pesto Sauce - Process in food processor
1 cup fresh basil   1 cup fresh grated Parmesan
½ cup olive oil   cheese
                                          ½ cup pistachio nuts

Garlic Cream - Process in food processor
1 (8-ounce) package cream cheese   ⅛ teaspoon pepper
¼ cup unsalted butter   ¼ cup pistachio nuts
1 clove garlic, pressed

- Spray loaf pan with olive oil spray and line with saran wrap.
- Add ingredients in the following layers: provolone, ½ pesto, provolone, all garlic cream, tomatoes, provolone, rest of pesto, provolone.
- Refrigerate several hours.
- Turn out of pan. Garnish with basil and cherry tomatoes.
- Serve with crackers.

Yield: 1 loaf

Artichoke-Filled French Bread

¼ cup margarine
2-3 cloves garlic, crushed
2 tablespoons sesame seeds
1 (14-ounce) can artichoke
   hearts, drained and chopped
1 cup shredded Monterey Jack
   cheese

1 cup grated Parmesan cheese
½ cup sour cream
1 (13 to 16-ounce) loaf French
   bread
½-1 cup shredded sharp Cheddar
   cheese

- Melt margarine in a large skillet. Add garlic and sesame seeds and cook until lightly browned.

- Remove from heat. Stir in artichokes and next 3 ingredients.

- Cover and refrigerate for 3 hours.

- Remove from refrigerator and let stand at room temperature for 10 minutes before assembling.

- Cut bread in half lengthwise. Cut out center, leaving ½-inch shell.

- Crumble removed pieces of bread and add to artichoke mixture.

- Spoon evenly into shells and sprinkle with Cheddar cheese. Can wrap tightly at this point and freeze for up to 3 weeks.

- Place on baking dish and cover with foil. Bake in 350° oven for 25 minutes. Uncover and bake for 8 minutes. Cut into ½-inch slices to serve.

Yield: 16 pieces

Jean T's Cheese Circles

½   pound margarine, softened
1   pound extra sharp Cheddar
    cheese, grated

3   cups plain flour
½   teaspoon salt
1   teaspoon cayenne

- With a strong mixer with bowl, cream margarine and cheese very well.
- Sift flour, salt and cayenne.
- Gradually add flour to margarine and cheese mixture, mix a little at a time, until all is very well blended and smooth. Will be very stiff.
- Place in a cookie press, using star point, make 2-inch circles on a cookie sheet until full.
- Bake at 350° for 10 to 12 minutes; do not let brown.
- Store in airtight container for several weeks.
- Can also be frozen for several weeks.

Yield: about 200

May Gray's Welcome Wafers

¾   cup butter, softened
⅓   cup crumbled blue cheese
½   cup grated sharp Cheddar
    cheese
2   cups sifted flour

½   clove garlic, minced
1   teaspoon parsley, dried
1   teaspoon chives, dried
    Powdered sugar, cayenne
    pepper, parsley

- Mix all ingredients thoroughly.
- Shape in 1½-inch diameter roll or rolls.
- Wrap in wax paper and chill thoroughly.
- Slice into ¼-inch slices and place on cookie sheet.
- Bake at 375° for 8 to 10 minutes.
- Dust with powdered sugar or sprinkle with cayenne pepper or parsley.

Yield: 4 dozen

Blue Cheese-Chutney Spread

2 (3-ounce) packages cream cheese
3 ounces blue cheese, crumbled
¼ cup butter or margarine, softened
¼ cup finely chopped onion
1-2 tablespoons milk
½ teaspoon curry powder
¼ teaspoon salt
3 tablespoons finely chopped chutney (any kind)

- Beat all ingredients except chutney until creamy.
- Stir in chutney.
- Pack into 2-cup crock or non-metal container; cover tightly.
- Refrigerate at least 24 hours, no longer than 2 weeks.
- Remove from refrigerator 1 hour before serving.
- Serve with crackers.

Yield: 2 cups

Sherry's Olive-Cheese Puffs

2 cups grated sharp Cheddar cheese
½ cup butter, softened
1½ cups sifted flour
½ teaspoon salt
1 teaspoon paprika
3-4 dozen stuffed small olives

- Blend cheese with butter.
- Stir in flour, salt and paprika. Mix well.
- Wrap 1 teaspoon of this mixture around each olive, covering it completely.
- Bake on a baking sheet in 400° oven for 10 to 15 minutes.

Yield: 36 to 48 appetizers

These may be frozen before baking by placing on cookie sheet. Freeze until firm; place in plastic bags and keep in the freezer for later use.

Marinated Cheese

½ cup olive oil	1 teaspoon sugar
½ cup white wine vinegar	¾ teaspoon basil
1 (2-ounce) jar diced pimento, drained	½ teaspoon salt
	½ teaspoon pepper
3 tablespoons chopped fresh parsley	1 (8-ounce) package cream cheese
	1 (8-ounce) package sharp Cheddar cheese
3 tablespoons minced green onion	
3 cloves garlic, minced	

- Combine first 10 ingredients in a jar and shake well.
- Cut cheeses in half lengthwise, then crosswise into ¼-inch thick blocks.
- Arrange cheese in three rows in a shallow container with a lid, alternating cheeses.
- Pour marinade over cheese. Cover and place in refrigerator for at least 8 hours.
- Transfer cheese to serving platter and spoon marinade on top.
- Serve with crackers.

Yield: serves approximately 16

Beautiful dish for the Christmas holidays. Delicious for anytime.

Triple Cheese Ball

½   pound sharp Cheddar cheese
¼   pound Roquefort or blue cheese
1   medium onion (optional)
1   (8-ounce) package cream
    cheese, softened

1   teaspoon garlic powder
1   tablespoon Worcestershire
    sauce
1   cup finely chopped pecans
1   cup chopped fresh parsley

- Process first 6 ingredients in food processor until smooth.
- Shape into 1 large ball or 1-inch balls and roll in parsley and pecans.
- Cover and refrigerate until serving.
- Serve with crackers.
- Best if made a day ahead. Freezes well.

Yield: 1 ball or 25 to 30 mini balls

If making mini balls, arrange cheese balls on serving plate to resemble a bunch of grapes. Add homemade pastry leaves or artificial grape leaves to make this look extra special.

Cheddar Carousel

1   pound sharp Cheddar cheese,
    grated
¾   cup mayonnaise
1   medium onion, finely chopped

1   clove garlic, pressed or
    ⅛ teaspoon garlic powder
½   teaspoon Tabasco sauce
1   cup chopped pecans
1   cup strawberry preserves

- Combine all ingredients except preserves and mix well.
- Pour into ring mold sprayed with cooking spray. Chill thoroughly.
- Unmold and fill center with preserves.
- Serve with crackers or small pumpernickel slices.

Yield: 10 to 12 servings

Hatcher Crackers

An easy and different snack.

40	Zesta saltine crackers
8	ounces extra sharp Cheddar cheese, grated

Cayenne pepper

- Line an oiled jellyroll pan with crackers.
- Sprinkle crackers with cayenne pepper - amount depends on desired hot flavor.
- Cover with grated cheese.
- Place on bottom rack of oven and broil until cheese is bubbly. WATCH CAREFULLY.
- Remove and allow crackers and oven to cool.
- Reheat oven to 150° and place pan or pans on top rack and leave overnight.
- Store in an airtight container.

Yield: 40 crackers

Toasted Parmesan Canapés

1	cup mayonnaise
½	cup grated Parmesan cheese
10	slices cooked bacon, crumbled
½	cup finely chopped onion

Dash Worcestershire sauce
12-24 slices thin white bread
Extra Parmesan cheese

- Mix first 5 ingredients together and refrigerate until ready to serve.
- Remove bread crusts and cut slices into 2 to 4 squares or rounds.
- Spread cheese mixture on each piece and sprinkle with additional cheese.
- Cook under broiler until puffy and browned.

Yield: 48 appetizers

Tomato Basil Appetizer

9-10	Roma tomatoes	¼	cup olive oil
8	ounces Havarti, smoked	¼	teaspoon salt
	Gouda, Havarti with dill or	¼	teaspoon pepper
	similar cheese		Baguette (fresh) or French
⅓	cup fresh basil		bread, sliced and toasted
2	cloves garlic		

- Cube tomatoes in ¼ to ½-inch cubes.
- Cube cheese in ¼-inch cubes.
- Cut fresh basil leaves in ⅛-inch strips.
- Crush garlic cloves.
- Mix above together in flat serving dish.
- Drizzle with olive oil. Sprinkle with salt and pepper.
- Cover and let sit at room temperature for 1 hour prior to serving.
- Uncover and serve with toasted baguette slices or crackers.
- Use a spoon or spoons so guests can serve themselves.

Yield: 8 appetizers

Jezebel Sauce

1	cup pineapple preserves	2	teaspoons dry mustard
1	cup apricot preserves	1¼	cups bottled horseradish
1	cup apple jelly	1	teaspoon salt
¼	cup vinegar		Cream cheese
1	tablespoon coarsely ground		Crackers
	black pepper		

- Mix all ingredients, except cream cheese and crackers, thoroughly.
- Refrigerate.
- Serve over cream cheese with crackers.

Yield: 5 cups

Will keep for months.

Hot Beef Dip

1	cup chopped pecans	1	teaspoon garlic salt
2	teaspoons butter	1	cup sour cream
2	(8-ounce) packages cream	4	tablespoons minced onion
	cheese, softened	2	dashes Worcestershire sauce
4	tablespoons milk		Crackers
5	ounces dried beef, minced		

- Toast pecans in butter and set aside.
- Mix all remaining ingredients and place in pie plate.
- Top with pecans.
- Bake for 20 minutes in a preheated 350° oven.
- Serve with crackers.

Yield: 12 servings

Can make and refrigerate ready to bake up to a day ahead of time.

Hot Crab Dip

2	(8-ounce) packages cream	1	pound backfin crabmeat
	cheese, softened	1	cup shredded sharp Cheddar
8	ounces sour cream		cheese
4	tablespoons mayonnaise	1	teaspoon Worcestershire sauce
½	teaspoon lemon juice		(optional)
1	teaspoon dry mustard	½	teaspoon horseradish (optional)
⅛	teaspoon garlic salt		Paprika

- Preheat oven to 325°.
- Blend all ingredients except crabmeat, ½ cup of cheese and paprika in a blender or mixer.
- Fold in crabmeat and pour into baking/serving dish.
- Bake at 325° for 45 minutes.
- Remove and top with remaining cheese. Sprinkle with paprika.
- Serve with crackers.

Yield: 5½ cups

Curry-Chutney Dip

2	(8-ounce) packages cream cheese, softened	½	teaspoon dry mustard
½	cup chutney	2	teaspoons curry powder

- Mix cream cheese with other ingredients.
- Refrigerate for several hours.
- Serve with crackers or fresh vegetables.

Yield: 2½ cups

Mexican Dip

2	(1-pound) cans whole peeled Italian tomatoes	2	(4-ounce) cans chopped green chiles
½	pound Velveeta cheese, cut in cubes	1-2	tablespoons chili powder
½	pound sharp Cheddar cheese, grated	1	teaspoon cumin (optional)

- Drain tomatoes 5 to 6 hours, chopping and stirring occasionally. Do not use food processor. They should be fairly dry but retain some moisture.
- In a casserole, layer Velveeta, Cheddar, chiles and spices.
- Spread tomatoes evenly over top.
- Cover and bake at 350° for 10 to 15 minutes and uncovered 10 to 15 minutes or until cheese is melted.
- Let sit 5 minutes, then stir thoroughly.
- Serve with tortilla chips or crackers.

Yield: 10 to 15 servings

May be frozen and heated in the microwave.

Shrimp Dip
Quick and easy.

1   (6½-ounce) can shrimp or
    1 cup fresh shrimp, peeled,
    boiled and coarsely chopped
1   (3-ounce) package cream
    cheese, softened

8   ounces sour cream
1   package dry Italian dressing
    mix

- Drain shrimp. Mix with other ingredients.
- Chill thoroughly before serving.
- Serve with crackers.

Yield: 2 cups

Kaki's Shrimp Appetizer

1   cup butter
1   (16-ounce) bottle Zesty Italian
    dressing

3   pounds shrimp, peeled and
    uncooked
    French bread, broken into
    chunks for dipping

- Melt butter and mix with Italian dressing.
- Put peeled, uncooked shrimp and butter mixture in 9 x 13-inch casserole dish.
- Bake at 350° for 20 minutes.
- Serve with picks for shrimp.
- Sauce is excellent for dipping bread.

Yield: 12 servings

Pizza Bites

2 (10-count) packages flaky style ¾ pound sharp Cheddar cheese,
    biscuits   grated
1 pound pork sausage   Grated Parmesan cheese
1 (15½-ounce) can pizza sauce

- Separate each biscuit into four layers.
- Place on ungreased cookie sheet and prick each piece with a fork.
- Bake at 300° for 10 minutes or until slightly brown.
- Cook sausage in skillet until crumbly and browned. Do not overcook. Drain on paper towels.
- Put 1 teaspoon of pizza sauce on each biscuit. Cover with 1 teaspoon of cooked sausage.
- Sprinkle with Cheddar cheese; then with Parmesan cheese. Can freeze at this point.
- Bake at 350° for 12 to 15 minutes or until bubbly.

Yield: 80 bites

Party Pork Tenderloin

1½ cups oil   ⅓ cup white wine vinegar
¾ cup soy sauce   1 clove garlic, crushed
1 tablespoon dry mustard   1 (1 to 2-pound) package pork
1 tablespoon black pepper   tenderloin
⅓ cup lemon juice

- Combine first 7 ingredients for marinade.
- Marinate pork overnight in refrigerator.
- Cook at 350° uncovered for 45 minutes.
- Slice thin and serve with rolls or party bread slices.

Yield: 48 appetizers

Manhattan Meatballs

2	pounds ground chuck	2	teaspoons salt
2	cups bread crumbs	2	tablespoons butter
½	cup chopped onion	½	cup bottled barbecue sauce
2	tablespoons dry parsley flakes	10	ounces apricot preserves
2	eggs		

- Mix first 6 ingredients and form into small balls.
- Sauté meatballs in butter until brown.
- Place in large casserole.
- Mix barbecue sauce and preserves.
- Spoon over meatballs.
- Bake at 350° for 35 minutes.
- Transfer to chafing dish and serve hot.

Yield: 100 meatballs

Bow Knots

1	loaf extra-thin sliced bread	12	bacon strips, uncooked and cut
1	(10¾-ounce) can cream of		in half
	celery soup		

- Trim crust from bread.
- Spread soup on bread slices, covering completely.
- Roll slice from corner to corner.
- Wrap bacon piece around each and secure with toothpick.
- Bake on cookie sheet at 250° for 1 hour or until dry and crisp.
- May be frozen and baked unthawed an extra 15 minutes.

Yield: 2 dozen

Bourbon Dogs

1	pound all-beef hot dogs	1½	cups ketchup
3/4	cup bourbon	½	cup brown sugar
1	tablespoon grated onion	1	tablespoon mustard

- Cut hot dogs into ½-inch slices.
- Place in heavy saucepan with other ingredients.
- Simmer on low heat for 45 minutes.
- Serve from a chafing dish with toothpicks.

Yield: 90 to 110 pieces

Picadillo

A hearty, spicy dip that men usually like.

1	pound ground beef	1	large jar diced pimento
1	pound ground pork	2	cloves garlic, minced
1	tablespoon oil	1	cup raisins
4	large fresh tomatoes or 1 (28-ounce) can, drained and chopped, save liquid	1	small can jalapeños, seeded and chopped
1	cup slivered almonds	1	teaspoon ground cumin
12	ounces tomato paste	1	teaspoon oregano

- Brown meats in oil in large skillet. Drain.
- Blanch fresh tomatoes; peel and dice.
- Add tomatoes to meats, may need to transfer to large saucepan at this point.
- Stir in remaining ingredients, cover and simmer for 20 to 30 minutes until raisins are plump and mixture is well blended.
- Serve with tortilla or corn chips.

Yield: 12 to 18 servings

Shrimp Sea Island

5	pounds shrimp, cooked and deveined	2	tablespoons sugar
5-10	mild white onions, sliced into thin rings	½	teaspoon salt
		¼	teaspoon Tabasco sauce
1	pint vegetable oil	2	tablespoons Worcestershire sauce
¾	pint cider vinegar	1	(3½-ounce) bottle of capers

- Place layer of shrimp in a large deep flat dish.
- Add a layer of onions and alternate shrimp and onions until all are used.
- Mix oil, vinegar, sugar, salt, Tabasco and Worcestershire thoroughly.
- Add capers, including juice and stir.
- Pour this mixture over shrimp.
- Cover and refrigerate for at least 12 hours. Stir occasionally.

Yield: 16 to 20 appetizers or 12 salads

Can be drained and served on lettuce leaf as a salad.

Rose's Crab Melt

1	(8-ounce) package cream cheese, softened		Tabasco sauce to taste
	Salt and pepper to taste	½	pound of crabmeat
1-2	tablespoons Worcestershire sauce	1	package English muffins, separated

- Mix cream cheese and next 3 ingredients.
- Fold in crabmeat.
- Spread on English muffins and cut into fourths.
- Can freeze at this point, thaw before baking.
- Bake at 350° for 20 minutes

Yield: 48 appetizers

Rum Punch

1	gallon brandy	2	dozen lemons, juiced
½	gallon heavy rum, light or dark		Sugar to taste
1	pint peach brandy	5-6	quarts carbonated water
2	quarts black tea		

- Mix all ingredients except carbonated water.
- Add carbonated water just before serving to strength of punch desired.
- Serve cold over crushed ice.

Yield: 130 (4-ounce) servings or 4 gallons

You may add 1 pint of maraschino cherries, sliced fresh strawberries or diced peaches.

Instant Party Punch

1	(48-ounce) can pink grapefruit juice	1	(15¼-ounce) can crushed pineapple
1	(48-ounce) can pineapple juice		Water
1	(48-ounce) can apple juice	1	(2-liter) ginger ale

- Chill all juices overnight.
- Put crushed pineapple and juice along with water in ring mold and freeze overnight.
- Pour all chilled juices into a large punch bowl and mix.
- Add ½ ginger ale.
- Float fruit ice ring.
- Add other ½ ginger ale.

Yield: 50 to 55 non-alcoholic or 65 with alcohol

Makes a good base for adding wine (2 bottles) or 1 fifth or the desired amount of vodka, rum or whiskey.

Wassail Bowl

1	orange	½	cup sugar
10	whole cloves	2	sticks cinnamon
2	bottles Claret wine		

- Cut orange in half, stick 5 cloves into skin of each half.
- Combine wine, cinnamon and sugar in a saucepan.
- Cover and simmer about 15 minutes.
- Pour into punch bowl. Float orange halves and serve hot.

Yield: 7 cups

Anne's Bloody Mary Mix

1	(46-ounce) can tomato juice	2	tablespoons celery salt
1	(46-ounce) can V-8 juice	6	ounces Rose's lime juice
5	ounces Worcestershire sauce	2	dashes lemon pepper
10-15	dashes Tabasco sauce	4	cups vodka
6	ounces whiskey sour liquid mix		

- Mix all ingredients, except vodka.
- Add vodka just before serving

Yield: 30 servings

Joyce's Special Champagne Punch

1	(15¼-ounce) can crushed pineapple	8	ounces amaretto
1	bottle champagne	24	ounces lemon-lime drink

- Blend and serve over cracked ice.

Yield: 8 servings

Supper Club Whiskey Sour Punch

1	(6-ounce) can frozen orange juice	3	(6-ounce) cans water
1	(6-ounce) can frozen limeade	3	(6-ounce) cans whiskey
1	(6-ounce) can frozen lemonade		Crushed ice

- One hour before serving, mix juices, water and whiskey and pour over crushed ice in a punch bowl.
- Can easily double or triple the recipe.

Yield: 8 to 10 servings

Vail Hot Spiced Wine

1	quart water	3	cinnamon sticks
2	cups sugar	½	lemon, peeled
25	whole cloves	½	gallon Burgundy wine

- Boil all ingredients except wine until syrupy.
- Simmer and add wine.
- Immediately remove from heat (do not let wine boil).
- Serve hot.

Yield: 15 servings

Sparkling Strawberry Mimosas

2½ cups orange juice   1   bottle dry champagne, chilled
1   (10-ounce) package frozen
    strawberries, partially thawed

- Combine juice and berries in blender and puree.
- Pour into pitcher and add champagne.
- Stir gently and garnish with strawberries, if desired.
- Serve immediately.

Yield: 8 servings

Gwyn's Favorite Tea

1   cup instant tea with lemon and   12   ounces pineapple juice
    sugar   Water
½   cup Tang

- Mix tea, Tang and pineapple juice in a 4-cup measuring cup.
- Add water to make 4 cups.
- Pour into 1-gallon container. Add 3 quarts of water.
- Chill.

Yield: 1 gallon

Keeps well and is a great thirst quencher!

Holiday Tea Punch

⅓	cup instant tea	1	(6-ounce) can frozen pink
2	cups water		lemonade
1	cup grenadine syrup	2	tablespoons lemon juice
2	cups cranberry juice cocktail	1	quart lemon-lime carbonated
2	(6-ounce) cans pineapple juice		beverage
			Decorative ice ring (optional)

- Combine all ingredients except carbonated beverage. Chill.
- Pour into a punch bowl. Add carbonated lemon-lime beverage.
- Add ice ring, if desired.

Yield: about 24 (4-ounce) servings

Coffee Punch

20	cups strong coffee	1	cup whipping cream, whipped
½	gallon vanilla ice cream,		(no substitute)
	softened	⅓	cup sugar

- Cool coffee to lukewarm.
- Mash ice cream in a punch bowl.
- Pour coffee over ice cream and stir.
- Top with sweetened whipped cream dollops.
- Can be decreased easily for a smaller group.

Yield: 20 to 25 servings

Hot Cranberry Tea

2	teaspoons nutmeg	12	cups hot water
2	teaspoons cinnamon	6	cups sugar
2	teaspoons allspice	4	cups orange juice
10	family-size tea bags	2	cups lemon juice
20	cups boiling water	2	gallons cranberry juice

- Tie spices in a bag and place spice and tea bags into boiling water.
- Cover and steep 10 minutes. Remove bags.
- Make syrup of hot water and sugar.
- Add remaining juices and syrup to spiced water.
- Serve hot.

Yield: 75 servings

Can make ahead to let flavors blend.

Breads, Breakfast and Brunch

Down East Color - Watercolor

Laura Davis Piner

Mrs. Piner is a Beaufort native and member of St. Paul's.
She majored in art at the University of North Carolina-Chapel Hill
and taught art in the public schools and community college.
She started the Mattie King Davis Gallery located on
the Beaufort Historic Grounds.

Orange Tea Bread or Sandwiches

1	large orange, sliced and unpeeled	1	cup white raisins, cranberries, or apricots
½	cup orange juice		
¼	cup butter, melted	2	cups flour
1	egg	1	teaspoon baking soda
1	cup sugar	½	teaspoon salt

Glaze

1	cup powdered sugar	1	tablespoon grated orange rind
½	cup orange juice		

Sandwich Filling

3	ounces soft cream cheese	1	teaspoon grated orange rind
2	tablespoons orange marmalade		

- Mix orange, juice, butter, egg, sugar and fruits in a blender.
- Add dry ingredients to above mixture in a bowl and blend well.
- Pour into loaf pan. Bake at 350° for 50 to 55 minutes.
- For glaze, punch holes in hot loaf and pour on glaze while still in pan.
- For sandwiches, mix cheese, marmalade and orange rind together and make small tea sandwiches. Slice bread thin.

Yield: 10 to 20 slices, depending on thickness

Bishop's Bread

2	cups flour	6	ounces chocolate chips
4	teaspoons baking powder	1	cup strong coffee
⅔	cup sugar	⅛	teaspoon baking soda
½	cup walnuts, chopped	1	egg, well beaten
½	cup dates, chopped	2	tablespoons vegetable oil

- Grease and flour 9-inch loaf pan.
- Mix flour, baking powder, sugar, walnuts, dates and chocolate chips.
- Add coffee, soda, egg and oil and mix well.
- Pour into pan and let stand for 20 minutes.
- Bake at 375° for 1 hour. Check after 40 minutes.
- Cool in pan for 20 minutes and then remove.

Yield: 1 loaf, doubles well

Pear Bread

3	cups flour	1	cup chopped pecans
1	teaspoon soda	¾	cup oil
1	teaspoon salt	3	eggs, slightly beaten
1	tablespoon cinnamon	2	cups sugar
¼	teaspoon baking powder	2	cups cooking pears, peeled and
2	teaspoons vanilla		grated or finely chopped

- Combine first 7 ingredients in large bowl.
- Make a well in center of above mixture.
- Combine oil, eggs, sugar and pears and place into well. Stir only until mixed.
- Pour into 2 greased and floured 9-inch loaf pans.
- Bake at 325° for 1 hour and 15 minutes.

Yield: 2 loaves

Cherry Sweet Bread

2½ cups sifted all-purpose flour
2 teaspoons baking powder
½ teaspoon soda
1 teaspoon salt
½ cup golden raisins
½ cup chopped red and green
    cherries
1 cup chopped walnuts

¾ cup butter, softened
1½ cups sugar
2 eggs
1 cup orange juice
    10X powdered sugar
    Milk
    Whole walnuts

- Sift together flour, baking powder, soda and salt.
- Sprinkle 1 cup of mixture over fruit and nuts in a separate bowl.
- Cream butter and sugar thoroughly. Add eggs and beat until light and fluffy.
- Add dry ingredients and orange juice. Stir until just blended.
- Fold in fruit and nuts.
- Spoon batter into well greased 9-inch tube pan.
- Bake in 350° oven for 1 hour or until center tests done.
- Cool 5 minutes and remove from pan.
- Frost top with 10X powdered sugar stirred with milk to make hard drizzle and garnish with whole walnuts.

Yield: 12 servings

Your favorite spices may be added as desired. Makes a pretty holiday cake.

Cardamom Banana Bread

⅔	cup raisins or dried currants	1	teaspoon ground cardamom
⅓	cup rum or apple cider	3	ripe bananas, mashed
1	cup unbleached white flour	⅓	cup canola or corn oil
¾	cup whole wheat flour	¾	cup brown sugar, firmly packed
2	teaspoons baking powder	2	eggs
1	teaspoon baking soda	½	cup chopped walnuts, lightly
1	teaspoon salt		toasted

- Preheat oven to 350° and grease a 9 or 10-inch loaf pan.
- Combine raisins and rum in saucepan, bring to simmer, turn off heat and let it sit for 10 minutes.
- Combine next 6 ingredients in large bowl and mix well.
- In another bowl combine banana, oil and sugar and beat with electric mixer for 1 minute.
- Add eggs and beat 1 minute.
- Pour banana mixture into flour mixture and mix until well combined.
- Stir in walnuts, then raisins and liquid.
- Pour into loaf pan and bake 50 to 60 minutes or until knife inserted comes out clean.
- Let cool in pan, remove and cool completely on rack.

Yield: 1 loaf or 4 mini loaves

Apple Carrot Muffins

2	eggs	1	tablespoon baking powder
2	egg whites	½	teaspoon soda
1¼	teaspoons Sweet 'n Low	¼	teaspoon salt
½	cup oil	1	teaspoon cinnamon
⅓	cup sugar	1	cup chopped apple
1	cup whole wheat flour	1	cup grated carrots
1	cup cake flour	1	teaspoon vanilla

- Mix eggs, egg whites, sugar substitute, oil and sugar in a large bowl.
- Mix flours, baking powder, soda, salt and cinnamon in another bowl.
- Fold dry ingredients into egg mixture.
- Stir in apples, carrots and vanilla.
- Put into greased or paper lined 2½-inch muffin tins.
- Bake at 375° for 20 to 25 minutes.

Yield: 16 muffins

Fran's Monkey Bread

1	tablespoon cinnamon	1	cup brown sugar
1	cup sugar		Chopped nuts (optional)
4	large cans biscuits		Chopped apples (optional)
1¼	sticks butter		

- Mix cinnamon and sugar.
- Cut each biscuit into quarters. Dip into sugar and cinnamon mix.
- Layer in a Bundt or tube pan.
- Melt butter and mix with brown sugar; pour over biscuits.
- Bake at 350° for 45 minutes.
- Add nuts or apples between layers if desired.
- Turn out onto serving platter and serve warm.

Yield: 12 to 15 servings

Pecan Muffins

2	tablespoons butter or margarine, melted	½	teaspoon baking soda
⅔	cup chopped pecans	½	teaspoon salt
1¾	cups sifted flour	½	cup sour cream
½	cup less 2 tablespoons sugar	½	cup peach or apricot preserves
1	teaspoon baking powder	1	egg
		1	teaspoon vanilla

- Preheat oven to 350° for pecan toasting.
- Combine pecans and butter- toast on baking sheet for 10 to 15 minutes, stirring every 4 to 5 minutes.
- Sift dry ingredients in large bowl.
- Combine sour cream, preserves, egg and vanilla. Add to dry ingredients. Add pecans. Stir just to combine.
- Fill greased muffin tins ⅔ full. Bake at 400° for 15 to 20 minutes until golden brown.
- Cool 10 minutes, then serve while warm.

Yield: 12 large muffins or 24 to 30 small muffins

Dot's Yeast Bread and Rolls

½	cup milk, scalded	¼	cup warm water (112°)
⅓	cup honey	2¾	cups bread flour (more or less
1½	teaspoons salt		depending on weather -
¼	cup canola oil		humidity)
¼	cup mashed potatoes	½	teaspoon grated lemon or
1	egg, slightly beaten		orange rind (optional)
2	teaspoons active dry yeast		

- Combine first 5 ingredients in a bowl, mix and cool to lukewarm. Stir in egg.
- Dissolve yeast in warm water and stir into milk mixture.
- Stir flour into mixture a little at a time, adding flour as needed to make stiff dough, beating well after each addition.
- Turn dough onto lightly floured board and knead until dough is smooth and elastic.
- Place dough in well greased bowl and let rise in a warm place until double in size (about 1 hour).
- Punch down. Let rest 10 minutes.
- Knead out air bubbles and form into either rolls (about 18) or 1 large loaf or 2 small loaves.
- Place rolls on lightly greased baking sheet. Place loaves in lightly greased loaf pans.
- Let rise until double (about 45 minutes).
- Bake at 350° until brown, about 15 to 20 minutes for rolls, 30 to 40 minutes for loaves.
- Remove from pans and cool on wire rack.

Yield: 1 large loaf , 2 small loaves or 18 rolls

For cinnamon rolls, roll dough out to ½-inch depth and cover with a mixture of ½ cup granulated sugar mixed with 2 tablespoons cinnamon. Roll up and cut into 1-inch slices to equal about 20 rolls. Place on lightly greased baking sheet. Allow to rise and bake at 350° until brown, about 15 to 20 minutes.

Substitute 1 cup of the bread flour with 1 cup of dark rye or wheat flour and use molasses instead of honey. You can also add 1 tablespoon of caraway seeds, anise seeds, or dill weed.

English Muffin Loaf

5	cups plain flour	¼	teaspoon baking soda
2	packages yeast	2	cups milk
1	tablespoon sugar	½	cup water
2	teaspoons salt		Cornmeal

- Combine first 5 ingredients in large bowl.
- Heat milk and water until very warm (120 to 130°).
- Add liquids to dry mixture and beat well by hand (batter will be sticky).
- Spoon into 2 (8-cup) loaf pans that have been greased and sprinkled with cornmeal.
- Sprinkle tops with cornmeal.
- Cover and let rise in a warm place until double in size.
- Bake at 400° for 20 minutes.
- Remove from pans immediately and cool.

Yield: 2 loaves

Whole recipe can be baked in a tube pan.

Heavenly Hot Cross Buns

1	cup milk, scalded	¾	teaspoon cinnamon
2	tablespoons butter	3	cups flour
¼	cup sugar or 3 tablespoons honey	2	eggs
½	teaspoon salt	¼	cup raisins, chopped or ¼ cup currants
1	package yeast, dissolved in ¼ cup lukewarm water	½	cup powdered sugar
		1	tablespoon milk

- Add butter, sugar and salt to milk and heat.
- When lukewarm, add dissolved yeast, cinnamon, flour and 1 egg and mix well.
- Add raisins. Cover and let rise until doubled.
- Roll out to 1-inch thickness. Cut into rounds, place on baking sheet 1-inch apart and let rise.
- Brush with 1 beaten egg.
- Cut a cross on top of each bun with a sharp knife.
- Bake at 375° for 20 minutes.
- Stir together powdered sugar and milk to make glaze.
- Remove from oven and fill crosses with powdered sugar glaze.

Yield: 24 buns

Streusel-Filled Coffee Cake

Cake

1½ cups all-purpose flour	¼ cup solid shortening
3 teaspoons baking powder	1 egg, well beaten
½ teaspoon salt	½ cup milk
¾ cup sugar	1 teaspoon vanilla

- Sift flour, baking powder, salt and sugar together.
- Cut in shortening until mixture is like fine cornmeal.
- Blend in egg, mix well with milk. Add vanilla and beat just enough to mix well.
- Prepare streusel filling.

Streusel Filling

2 tablespoons flour	2 tablespoons butter, melted
½ cup brown sugar	½ cup chopped nuts
2 teaspoons cinnamon	

- Mix flour, sugar and cinnamon.
- Blend in melted butter and stir in chopped nuts.
- Alternate layers of batter and streusel in greased and floured 9-inch cake pan.
- Bake 25 to 30 minutes in 350° oven.

Yield: 6 servings

Can be easily doubled.

Sour Cream Coffee Cake

	Butter	1	teaspoon baking powder
8	pecan halves	1/8	teaspoon salt
2	sticks butter or margarine, softened	1	cup sour cream
		1/2	teaspoon vanilla
2	cups sugar	1/2	cup chopped pecans
2	eggs	2	tablespoons sugar
2	cups sifted cake flour	1	teaspoon cinnamon

- Generously coat a 12-cup Bundt pan with butter. Place a little extra butter in each crease of pan and press a pecan half into each crease.
- Cream butter and sugar in a large mixing bowl. Beat in eggs.
- Sift flour, baking powder and salt and gradually add to creamed mixture, blending well.
- Carefully fold in sour cream and vanilla.
- Mix chopped nuts, sugar and cinnamon and sprinkle 2 tablespoons on bottom of pan.
- Cover with 1/3 of cake batter. Alternate nut mixture and batter in pan, ending with topping.
- Bake at 350° for 55 to 60 minutes.

Yield: 12 servings

Angel Biscuits

5	cups self-rising flour	1	package yeast, dissolved in
¼	cup sugar		2 tablespoons warm water
¾	cup solid shortening	2	cups buttermilk
			Melted butter

- Sift flour. Add sugar. Cut in shortening.
- Add yeast that has been dissolved in warm water. Add buttermilk and knead lightly.
- Place in refrigerator several hours or overnight.
- Preheat oven to 425°.
- Turn out onto a lightly floured board and roll dough out to ⅓-inch thickness.
- Cut with 2-inch biscuit cutter.
- Prick biscuits with a fork and brush with melted butter.
- Bake 12 to 15 minutes.

Yield: about 80 biscuits

Anne's Parmesan Biscuits

No one will guess these are canned biscuits!

1	(10-count) can Hungry Jack Biscuits	¾	cup butter, melted
		¾	cup grated Parmesan cheese

- Separate biscuits and press out flat. Cut in half.
- Dip both sides in melted butter.
- Dip into Parmesan cheese.
- Fold over and place on ungreased cookie sheet.
- Bake as directed on can.

Yield: 20 biscuits

Bite-Size Brunch Biscuits

2	cups flour	6	tablespoons solid shortening
3	teaspoons baking powder	⅔	cup buttermilk
1	teaspoon salt		

- Mix dry ingredients. Cut in shortening.
- Add buttermilk. Mix well.
- Roll on floured surface and cut into 50-cent piece size circles.
- Bake at 400° until golden brown.

Yield: 30 to 40 biscuits

Mexican Cornbread

1	cup self-rising cornmeal	1½	cups shredded sharp Cheddar cheese
½	teaspoon soda		
½	teaspoon salt	1	teaspoon garlic powder
½	teaspoon sugar	1	(7-ounce) can whole kernel corn
3	eggs, well beaten	1	(2-ounce) jar chopped pimento, drained
1	cup buttermilk		
3	jalapeño peppers, seeded and chopped	½	cup bacon drippings or canola oil
½	cup chopped onion	½	cup bacon bits (optional)

- Combine cornmeal, soda, salt and sugar.
- Stir in remaining ingredients and spoon into a well greased 2-quart baking dish or 10-inch iron skillet.
- Bake at 350° for 45 minutes or until golden brown.

Yield: 12 servings

Double Deluxe Cornbread

1	(8½-ounce) box corn muffin mix	2	eggs, beaten
½	cup butter or margarine, melted	1	cup cream-style corn
1	cup sour cream	1	cup whole kernel corn, drained

- Mix all ingredients well.
- Pour into greased 9 x 9-inch baking pan.
- Bake at 400° for 40 minutes or until browned and firm.

Yield: 9 to 12 servings

"Ginny Gordon's Gifts and Gadgets" Fried Cornbread

2	medium ears yellow corn	1	egg, beaten
½	cup Bisquick		Milk (enough for thick batter)
2	tablespoons sugar	⅓	teaspoon nutmeg
½	teaspoon salt		Crisco
¼	teaspoon black pepper		

- Cut corn from ears into mixing bowl; scrape ears and add juice.
- Add all other ingredients to make thick batter.
- Heat enough Crisco at medium heat to cover bottom of frying pan.
- Drop batter ⅛-cup at a time (as you would pancakes).
- Remove and keep warm in 150° oven until ready to serve.

Yield: 8 servings

Fresh uncooked yellow corn makes the difference.

Halifax Cornbread

2	eggs, well beaten		Dash salt
½	cup liquid oil	1	cup cream-style corn
¾	cup buttermilk	1	cup self-rising cornmeal
¼	teaspoon soda	½	cup grated sharp Cheddar
1	small onion, chopped		cheese

- Combine all ingredients, except cheese.
- Pour ½ of batter into greased 9 x 9-inch dish.
- Sprinkle cheese over batter. Pour in rest of batter.
- Bake 30 minutes at 350°.

Yield: 12 servings

Squash Cornbread

1	(8½-ounce) box corn muffin mix	1	small onion, chopped
1	stick butter, melted	2	cups finely chopped fresh
4	eggs, beaten		yellow squash
1	cup buttermilk	1	teaspoon salt

- Mix all ingredients.
- Pour in greased 9 x 13-inch dish.
- Bake at 400° for 20 minutes.

Yield: 12 to 15 servings

Pumpkin Bread

4	eggs	1	cup whole wheat flour
1	cup sugar	2	teaspoons soda
2	cups brown sugar	2½	teaspoons salt
1	cup vegetable oil	1	teaspoon cinnamon
2	cups canned pumpkin	1	teaspoon nutmeg
⅔	cup water	1	cup raisins
2	cups plain flour	½	cup chopped pecans

- Mix eggs, sugars and oil with mixer. Add pumpkin and water and blend well.
- Add dry ingredients and mix thoroughly with mixer.
- Pour into 2 greased loaf pans.
- Bake at 350° for 50 to 60 minutes. Test for doneness.
- Cool completely in pans, then remove and cool on rack 1 more hour.

Yield: 2 loaves

Vegetable Tea Sandwiches

8	ounces cream cheese, softened	¼	cup finely chopped onion
¾	cup finely chopped pecans, toasted	3	hard-boiled eggs, chopped
			Dash pepper
¼	cup finely chopped green pepper	¾	teaspoon salt
			Bread

- Mix well and spread on any type bread.
- Cut into small tea size sandwiches.
- Spread can be refrigerated for up to a week.

Yield: 24 sandwiches, 2½ to 3 cups

Eight Veggie Sandwich Spread

1	stalk celery	16	ounces cream cheese, softened
1	carrot	½	teaspoon dry mustard
2	cauliflower florets	½	teaspoon cayenne pepper
½	medium onion	1	teaspoon salt
1	stalk broccoli (stalk only)	½	teaspoon ginger
½	green pepper	¾	teaspoon dill weed
1	small yellow squash	1½	teaspoons Worcestershire sauce
½	cucumber, unpeeled and seeded	¼	cup Ranch dressing
⅓	cup black olives		(approximately)

- Prepare vegetables first. Chop all very fine and set aside - should be about 2 cups firmly packed to equal 1 pound. Should be a balanced mixture but add more or less onion to taste.

- Place cream cheese in large mixing bowl and add all dry ingredients and Worcestershire sauce and mix well.

- Add ½ Ranch dressing and mix well.

- Add chopped vegetables and mix thoroughly.

- Add remaining dressing until mixture is spreadable consistency.

- Adjust seasonings to your taste. Should have a bit of a bite.

- Cover and chill several hours or overnight.

- Spread on bread for sandwiches or serve with crackers.

Yield: 4 cups, 16 sandwiches, or 3 to 4 dozen tea sandwiches

One of our best sellers at the Old Homes Tour Lunch sponsored by St. Paul's ECW, served on homemade breads.

Pimento Cheese Sandwich Spreads

Homemade

10 ounces sharp Cheddar cheese, grated	4 ounces diced pimento, drained
8 ounces cream cheese, softened	½ cup mayonnaise (more or less)

- Blend all ingredients until smooth and spreadable.

Yield: 3 cups

Kaye's Pimento Cheese

10 ounces sharp Cheddar cheese, grated	4 ounces sweet pickle relish
4 ounces diced pimento, drained	Dash onion salt
	Salad dressing

- Mix cheese, pimento and relish until blended, then add salt.
- Add salad dressing to desired consistency.

Yield: 2¼ cups

Verta's Party Pimento for A Crowd

16 ounces extra sharp Cheddar cheese, grated	2 (7-ounce) jars diced pimento with liquid
16 ounces sharp Cheddar cheese, grated	1 tablespoon sugar
24 ounces cream cheese, softened	Cayenne pepper to taste
	3-4 cups mayonnaise

- Mix all ingredients until well blended and spreadable.

Yield: 8 quarts

Grandma's Pancakes

1	cup buttermilk	1	teaspoon baking soda
1	egg	1	tablespoon butter, melted
1	cup flour		Vegetable oil
1	tablespoon sugar		

- Mix buttermilk and egg.
- Add dry ingredients and whisk into buttermilk and egg mixture. Add melted butter and mix.
- Drop ½ cup batter on to hot griddle or heavy frying pan moistened with vegetable oil or butter.
- Turn when top of pancake begins to bubble.

Yield: 2 to 3 servings

Company French Toast

4	ounces cream cheese, softened	2	eggs
6	tablespoons strawberry preserves (all-fruit type)	¼	cup milk
		1-2	tablespoons butter
8	slices sourdough bread or other thick sliced bread		Powdered sugar

- Combine cream cheese and preserves in small bowl until smooth.
- Place spread on 4 bread slices and cover with remaining 4 slices to make sandwiches.
- Beat eggs and milk in shallow dish.
- Melt 1 tablespoon of butter in skillet.
- Dip each side of sandwiches in egg mixture.
- Cook sandwiches in skillet, turning until brown on both sides.
- Add butter to skillet as needed.
- Sprinkle with sugar and serve immediately.

Yield: 4 servings

Easy Breakfast Casserole

A real hit with children!

1	pound hot sausage	8	ounces grated sharp Cheddar cheese
6	eggs		
2	(8-ounce) packages refrigerated crescent rolls		Butter
			Sesame seeds

- Cook sausage and drain. Scramble eggs.
- Place 1 package crescent rolls flat into 9 x 13-inch casserole dish. Seal seams.
- Layer sausage, eggs and then cheese in order.
- Place remaining package of crescent rolls on top to form crust and seal edges.
- Dot with butter and sesame seeds.
- Bake at 375° for 20 minutes until brown.

Yield: 12 servings

Shrimp and Cheese Strata

A great brunch or main dish.

6	slices white bread	¼	cup butter, melted
½	pound Old English cheese or extra sharp cheese	3	eggs, beaten
1	pound shrimp, cooked and cut into pieces	½	teaspoon dry mustard
		½	teaspoon salt
		1	pint milk

- Cut bread and cheese into cubes.
- In an 8 x 11-inch greased casserole, layer shrimp, bread and cheese. Pour melted butter over layers.
- Blend together eggs, mustard, salt and milk. Pour over first mixture.
- Let stand overnight in refrigerator.
- Bake at 350° for 1 hour, covered.

Yield: 6 to 8 servings

Sausage and Cheese Puff

A great breakfast or brunch make ahead casserole!

	Butter, softened	1½-2	cups shredded sharp Cheddar
6-8	slices white bread, crust		cheese
	removed	4	eggs
1	pound mild or hot sausage,	1½	cups milk
	browned, crumbled and	1	teaspoon salt
	drained	½	teaspoon pepper
		½	teaspoon dry mustard

- Spread butter on bread. Cut into quarters and line 8 x 11-inch greased casserole.

- Spread sausage over bread and then sprinkle cheese over sausage.

- Beat eggs and remaining ingredients until fluffy.

- Pour over bread and sausage. Cover and refrigerate overnight.

- Uncover and bake at 350° for 30 minutes. Serve hot.

Yield 6 to 8 servings

1½ to 2 cups diced ham may be substituted for sausage.

Southern Grits Casserole

1½ cups grits	1½ cups orange juice
4 cups boiling water	(fresh, if possible)
1½ teaspoons salt	5 eggs, slightly beaten
½ teaspoon grated orange rind	Orange slices
6 tablespoons butter or margarine	Sugar

- Pour grits into boiling water. Add salt and orange rind.

- Stir grits constantly until mixture is thickened but not dry. Remove from heat.

- Add butter and orange juice, stirring until well blended.

- Gently stir in eggs.

- Spoon into greased 2½-quart casserole.

- Bake at 350° for 55 minutes or until knife comes out clean when inserted from the middle of the casserole.

- Garnish with fresh orange slices and sprinkle with sugar.

Yield: 6 to 8 servings

"Cousins Bed and Breakfast"
Mexican Grits

Even people who hate grits like this recipe!

2	tablespoons olive oil	1	(10¾-ounce) can Cheddar cheese soup
1	medium onion, chopped		
½	bell pepper, chopped	1	soup can water
1	teaspoon minced garlic	1	teaspoon Satan's Breath hot chili powder
1	(4-ounce) can mushrooms, drained		
1	(7-ounce) can Mexican corn, undrained	1	tablespoon Satan's Breath Cajun blend
1	(14½-ounce) can diced tomatoes with chiles, undrained	1	teaspoon each salt and pepper
		2½	cups instant grits
1	tablespoon each Worcestershire sauce and soy sauce	½	cup shredded New York extra sharp Cheddar cheese

- Place olive oil in 3-quart saucepan and heat over medium heat.
- Add onion, pepper and garlic and cook until onion is clear.
- Add mushrooms, corn, tomatoes, Worcestershire sauce and soy sauce and stir.
- When temperature is back up, add soup, water, spices and grits.
- Fold in shredded cheese and stir. Cover and remove from heat.
- Let rest 5 to 10 minutes. Keep warm until ready to serve.
- If too thick, add hot water.

Yield: 10 servings

Satan's Breath products are their registered trademark but you may substitute your favorite chili powder or Cajun flavoring.

Grits Logs Olé

3	cups water	½	cup flour
1	teaspoon salt	6	tablespoons butter or oil
1	cup grits		Salsa
1	egg, beaten		

- Cook grits according to directions.
- Pour into lightly greased 8 x 8-inch pan.
- Chill thoroughly in refrigerator overnight.
- Cut grits into 1½ x 4-inch strips or logs.
- Dip in egg; dust with flour and sauté in butter or oil until brown.
- Serve with salsa.

Yield: 8 servings

Great for left over grits. A breakfast dish, side dish, or appetizer.

Soups and
Stews

Grand Old Lady - Pastel

Millie Voorhees

Mrs. Voorhees resides in Morehead City and is a former member of St. Paul's. Married to an artist, Ed Voorhees, now deceased, she began painting after her children were grown, studying at the Art Students League in New York. She has shown her work nationally and has won numerous awards. Mrs. Voorhees works primarily in watercolor and oils.

Crab Bisque

2	sticks butter or margarine	1	quart half-and-half
3	tablespoons chicken base	½	teaspoon white pepper
1	cup flour	¼	cup dried parsley
2	quarts milk	1	pound backfin crabmeat

- Melt butter in heavy stockpot over medium heat.
- Add chicken base, stirring until blended.
- Add flour and stir until very smooth and mixture bubbles.
- Add milk, half-and-half, white pepper and parsley.
- Continue cooking over medium heat, stirring constantly until mixture is smooth and boils for 2 minutes.
- Gently add crabmeat and heat until mixture just begins to simmer.
- Remove from heat and serve.

Yield: 12 servings

Fish Stew

½	cup salt pork drippings	1-2	red pepper pods
5	pounds potatoes	2	cans Herring Roe
5	pounds onions	2	(10¾-ounce) cans tomato soup
5	pounds fish (rock or flounder)	1	dozen eggs
	Salt and pepper to taste		

- Place pork drippings in large pot. Peel potatoes and onions and slice round.
- Layer potatoes, onions and fish on top of drippings. Add salt and pepper to taste. Add red pepper pods and roe.
- Mix soup with enough water to cover mixture. Do not stir.
- Bring to a boil, reduce heat to medium and cook until vegetables are tender.
- Break eggs around top of stew and continue cooking until they are hard.

Yield: 8 to 10 servings

North River Seafood Bisque

1 stick butter or margarine	½ tablespoon Worcestershire
1 medium onion, finely chopped	sauce
1 large rib celery, finely chopped	1 quart half-and-half
½ pound scallops, cut if large	1 (6½-ounce) can clams and juice
½ pound shrimp, peeled and	1 (4½-ounce) can crabmeat,
boiled, cut into pieces	drained or 6 ounces fresh
½ cup flour	crabmeat
1¼ teaspoons dry mustard	¼ teaspoon nutmeg
1½ teaspoons salt	1½ tablespoons brandy or white
½ teaspoon cayenne pepper	wine
(to taste)	Paprika

- In a 2-quart saucepan, melt butter.
- Add vegetables and cook until almost limp.
- Add scallops and cook until white, then add shrimp.
- Add flour (more if you like it thicker) and stir well.
- Add mustard, salt, pepper and Worcestershire sauce.
- Gradually stir in half-and-half, stirring until thickened (do not let it boil).
- Add clams, stirring constantly and then fold in crabmeat and nutmeg.
- Stir in brandy or wine; adjust seasonings to your taste.
- Ladle into bowls and dust with paprika.

Yield: 6 to 8 servings

Frogmore Stew

5-6	quarts water
1	teaspoon salt
¼	cup or 1 package seafood boil (Old Bay)
2	onions, sliced
2	pounds hot sausage, cut into 2-inch slices

4	pounds small red potatoes, scrubbed
6-8	ears fresh corn, broken in half
3-4	pounds fresh shrimp, unpeeled
	Butter
	Cocktail sauce
	Tartar sauce

- Bring water and salt to full boil in large stockpot.
- Add seafood seasoning and boil 4 to 5 minutes.
- Add onion and sausage and boil for 5 minutes. Remove seasoning bag.
- Add whole potatoes; reduce heat to medium and cook until tender.
- Add corn and cook about 6 to 10 minutes. Add shrimp and cook until pink, about 3 to 4 minutes.
- Remove all from water and serve immediately with butter and sauces.

Yield: 8 servings

A complete meal! Everything can be arranged on a large platter or in individual bowls. Just add slaw or fresh tomatoes, cucumbers and cornbread for a delightful summer supper.

Oysters Rockefeller Stew

2	slices bacon	¾	pint shucked oysters with
½	cup thinly sliced leeks		liquor
½	cup thinly sliced celery	1	teaspoon Worcestershire sauce
1	clove garlic, minced	1½	cups packed thinly sliced raw
	Pinch cayenne pepper		spinach leaves
2½	cups whole milk or half-and-half		Salt and pepper to taste

- Fry bacon in heavy saucepan until crisp. Drain, crumble and reserve.

- Pour off all but 1 tablespoon of drippings. Add leeks, celery and garlic to drippings.

- Sauté over medium heat for 6 to 8 minutes until softened.

- Add cayenne pepper, then milk and bring to simmer.

- Add oysters (cut up any large ones) and Worcestershire sauce and return to simmer.

- Add spinach and simmer about 2 minutes until spinach is wilted and oysters cooked through.

- Season with salt and pepper to taste.

- Ladle into 2 bowls and top with bacon bits.

Yield: 2 servings

Recipe can be doubled or tripled easily.

Robert's Conch Chowder

2	quarts water	1	jalapeño pepper, seeded and chopped
1	quart conchs, cleaned and cut into small pieces		Dash red pepper
1½	pounds onions, chopped		Salt and pepper to taste
2	cups chopped celery	2	pounds potatoes, peeled and diced
½	cup cold bacon grease	1	cup regular grind white cornmeal

- Put all ingredients, except potatoes and cornmeal, in large pot with water.
- Simmer until tender, approximately 3 to 4 hours.
- Add potatoes and cook until tender.
- Add cornmeal and thicken to taste.

Yield: 8 servings

Jarrett Bay Clam Chowder

4	slices bacon, cut into ¼-inch pieces	4	cups clam juice
2	medium onions, chopped	2	cups water
3	cups chopped clams	4	cups diced potatoes
			Salt and pepper to taste

- Sauté bacon in large pot until almost cooked.
- Add onions and cook until transparent.
- Add clams, juice and water and bring to boil.
- Reduce heat and simmer covered for about 30 minutes.
- Add potatoes and simmer until done, about 30 minutes.

Yield: 8 to 10 servings

Even better the next day.

Cioppino (Seafood Stew)

1	large onion, chopped	1	teaspoon basil
1	medium green pepper, chopped		Salt and pepper to taste
½	cup chopped celery	1	pound shrimp, peeled
1	carrot, pared and shredded	1	dozen clams, in shell
3	cloves garlic, minced	1½	cups dry white wine
3	tablespoons olive oil	1	pound scallops
2	(15-ounce) cans diced tomatoes	1	pound crabmeat
1	(8-ounce) can tomato sauce	2	tablespoons fresh parsley
1	bay leaf		

- In a large soup pot, sauté onion, pepper, celery, carrot and garlic in oil until soft.

- Stir in tomatoes, tomato sauce, bay leaf, basil, salt and pepper. Heat to boiling. Cover and simmer for 2 hours; discard bay leaf.

- Scrub clams under running water to remove all mud and sand.

- Stir wine into sauce, add shrimp and scallops; simmer covered 7 to 10 minutes.

- Place clams in a layer on top of sauce; cover and steam 10 to 15 minutes or until clams are fully open (discard any unopened ones).

- Add crabmeat and cook 5 more minutes.

- Ladle into bowls and sprinkle with parsley.

Yield: 4 to 6 servings

If clams are not available, use 1 bottle of clam juice and increase other seafood. Sauce can be made a day before. Add wine and seafood right before serving.

Connie Mason's Stew for a Crowd

1	tablespoon bacon drippings	½	cup chopped parsley
1	(8-ounce) package frozen lima or butter beans	2	large garlic cloves, chopped
	Water	4	cups chicken stock
4	tablespoons butter	½	pound lump crabmeat, picked
1	medium white onion, chopped	5	pounds shrimp, cooked, peeled, deveined and coarsely chopped
1	cup chopped scallions		
½	cup chopped celery	1	quart half-and-half

- Heat large heavy saucepan over high heat.
- Add bacon drippings and beans and stir to coat.
- Add water just to cover and boil.
- Reduce heat and simmer until beans are tender (about 30 minutes).
- Drain beans and cool; place in food processor and blend until smooth. Set aside.
- Melt butter in 6½-quart stockpot over medium high heat.
- Add onions, scallions and celery and cook until tender but not brown. Reduce heat if necessary.
- Add parsley and garlic and cook until aroma of garlic is released.
- Add bean puree and chicken stock; bring to slow boil and simmer 10 minutes.
- Add crabmeat, shrimp and half-and-half.
- Bring mixture to slow boil and simmer about 5 minutes or until heated through, occasionally stirring carefully.
- Serve immediately.

Yield: 25 servings

Newport River Seafood Gumbo

¼	pound butter	2	pounds fresh shrimp, peeled
4	tablespoons flour		and deveined
2	quarts water	2	pounds fresh fish, skinned and
5	fresh tomatoes, finely chopped		boned
2	pounds fresh okra, sliced		Salt and pepper to taste
1	pound fresh crabmeat		Rice
1	pint fresh oysters		

- Melt butter and add flour, making a smooth paste, stirring constantly over medium heat until roux is a rich brown (careful not to burn).

- Add water, slowly stirring until all is blended.

- Add tomatoes and okra. Cook slowly for 1 hour on low to medium heat.

- Add crabmeat, oysters, shrimp and fish.

- Return to slow boil and cook 15 minutes.

- Gumbo should be thick and ready to serve over rice.

Yield: 8 servings

If cooked a few hours ahead, reheat slowly and stir often to keep from sticking.

Tortilla Soup

½	cup chopped celery	1	teaspoon chili powder or
3	cloves garlic, minced or pressed		3 serrano chiles, chopped
1	medium onion, chopped	6-8	cups tortilla chips
¼	cup chopped parsley	1	cup grated sharp Cheddar
1	tablespoon olive oil		cheese
1	pound ground beef		Chopped avocados
1	(14½-ounce) can Italian		Chives
	tomatoes		Chopped chiles
4	(14½-ounce) cans chicken		Tabasco sauce
	broth		Chopped onion
			Sour cream

- Sauté celery, garlic, onion and parsley in oil.
- Add beef and cook until brown. Add tomatoes and mix.
- In a soup pot, heat broth until almost boiling.
- Add above mixture and chili powder and bring to boil.
- Reduce heat and simmer for 15 to 20 minutes, stirring to blend well.
- To serve, place ½ to 1 cup chips in soup bowls. Add soup and sprinkle with cheese. Offer avocado, chives, chiles, Tabasco sauce, onion and sour cream as soup toppings.

Yield: 6 to 8 servings.

Five Hour Busy Day Stew

Great for bridge or meeting days.

2-2½ pounds beef stew meat, cut up
1 cup chopped celery
2 cups sliced carrots
2 medium to large onions, chopped
4 medium potatoes, diced
1 (10¾-ounce) can tomato soup or 1 (14½-ounce) can seasoned tomatoes

1½ soup cans water
1 tablespoon Worcestershire sauce
1 tablespoon sugar
2 tablespoons tapioca
Salt and pepper to taste

- Put meat and vegetables in a roaster or large casserole with cover.

- Mix soup, water, Worcestershire sauce, sugar, tapioca and seasonings. Pour over meat and vegetables.

- Cover tightly with foil, then add lid. Bake in preheated 275° oven for 5 hours or longer. Do not lift lid.

Yield: 4 to 6 servings

Mediterranean Beef Stew
with Sun-Dried Tomatoes and Olives

2	pounds lean beef stew meat	⅛	teaspoon crushed red pepper
2	tablespoons olive oil	½	cup water
2	medium onions, sliced	⅓	cup quartered and pitted
3	garlic cloves, thinly sliced		Kalamata olives
¾	cup dry vermouth	⅓	cup sun-dried tomato strips
1	(28-ounce) can tomatoes,	½	cup lightly packed fresh basil
	chopped, juice reserved		leaves, shredded
2	teaspoons balsamic vinegar		Rice or noodles
¼	teaspoon black pepper		

- Pat meat dry. Cook in oil in large stew pot over medium heat until brown; remove to plate.

- Add onions to oil and cook until golden, add garlic and cook 1 minute.

- Pour in vermouth and boil about 1 to 2 minutes until reduced by half.

- Add tomatoes and juice, vinegar, peppers and ½ cup water.

- Add meat and its juices. Bring to boil then reduce to low, cover and simmer about 1¼ hours.

- Add olives and simmer 30 more minutes.

- Add sun-dried tomatoes and simmer 5 minutes. Can be made to this point up to 2 days in advance.

- Just before serving, stir in fresh basil. Serve with rice or noodles.

Yield: 4 to 6 servings

Low Country Chicken Gumbo

1	(4-pound) whole chicken, cut into pieces	1	pound smoked sausage, cut into ¼-inch pieces
1	onion, quartered	3	tomatoes, peeled and chopped
	Celery leaves	1	garlic cloves, minced
1	teaspoon salt	1	(16-ounce) can tomato puree
6	slices bacon	1	(10-ounce) package frozen corn
2	large onions, chopped	1	(10-ounce) package frozen okra
2	green peppers, chopped	1	teaspoon dried thyme
2	stalks celery, chopped		Rice

- Combine first 4 ingredients in 4-quart pot and add water to cover.

- Simmer 40 to 45 minutes until tender.

- Remove chicken and reserve broth, straining it. Cut chicken into bite-size pieces.

- Cook bacon until crisp, drain, crumble, set aside. Reserve 1 tablespoon fat and add onion, peppers and celery and cook until tender.

- Add sausage, chicken, vegetables and all other ingredients including strained broth.

- Simmer for 2 hours; serve over rice with crumbled bacon.

Yield: 10 servings

Freezes well.

Brunswick Stew

1 large onion, chopped	1 (15-ounce) can whole kernel
1 large green pepper, chopped	corn with red and green
1 cup frozen sliced okra	peppers, drained
2 cups frozen cubed hash brown	1 (15-ounce) can lima beans,
potatoes	drained
1½ cups barbecued or cooked	2 cups chicken broth
chopped pork	½ teaspoon salt
1 cup chopped cooked chicken	½ teaspoon pepper
1 (14-ounce) can diced tomatoes	¼ teaspoon Worcestershire sauce
1 (15-ounce) can tomato sauce	

- Combine all ingredients in a 5-quart slow cooker.
- Cook on high, covered, for 6½ hours.
- Reduce heat to low until ready to serve.

Yield: 14 cups

To cook on top of stove, use heavy stew pot, bring to a boil, then reduce heat and simmer 2½ to 3 hours, stirring frequently.

Festive Black Bean Chili

2	cups chopped onions	2	(15-ounce) cans black beans,
2	cloves garlic, minced or pressed		drained and rinsed
½	cup water	3	cups fresh tomatoes or
1	tablespoon ground cumin		1 (28-ounce) can whole
1	tablespoon ground coriander		tomatoes with juice
1	cup prepared Mexican-style	2	cups fresh corn or 1 (10-ounce)
	salsa, red		package frozen corn kernels
2	red and/or green bell peppers,		Salt to taste
	chopped	¼	cup fresh cilantro, chopped

- In a heavy soup pot, cook onions and garlic in water on high heat, stirring frequently, about 5 minutes.
- Add cumin and coriander and stir for 1 minute.
- Stir in salsa and peppers, lower heat, cover and simmer 5 minutes.
- Add tomatoes and beans; simmer 20 minutes stirring occasionally.
- Add corn and simmer 20 minutes. Add salt, Tabasco and cilantro.

Yield: 4 to 6 servings

Trim Turkey Chili

1	teaspoon olive oil	1	tablespoon lime juice
1	medium onion, chopped	2	teaspoons chili powder
1	clove garlic, minced		(or more to taste)
1	(28-ounce) can tomatoes, undrained	1½	teaspoons each dried oregano and cumin seeds
1	(15½-ounce) can red kidney beans, undrained	1	cup turkey broth, fat skimmed
1	cup chopped celery	1	cup diced cooked turkey
1	large green bell pepper, seeded and chopped	6	tablespoons shredded light cheese
1	(4-ounce) can chopped green chili peppers, drained	2	tablespoons chopped fresh cilantro or parsley

- Preheat oil in a large cooking pot or Dutch oven.

- Add onions and garlic and cook until onions are soft, stirring frequently.

- Add tomatoes, kidney beans, celery, bell and chili peppers, lime juice, chili powder, oregano and cumin seeds.

- Cover and simmer for 1½ hours.

- Add broth; simmer uncovered 30 minutes more. Stir in turkey and heat through.

- Serve in bowls and sprinkle with cheese and cilantro.

Yield: 6 servings

White Chili

2	(14½-ounce) cans chicken broth	1	(4-ounce) can chopped green chiles
2	(15-ounce) cans white beans, drained	1	teaspoon cumin
3	cups chopped cooked chicken breasts	¾	teaspoon oregano
1	medium onion, chopped	¼	teaspoon ground red pepper
1	(16-ounce) package frozen white corn, thawed	1	cup salsa
		¼	cup sour cream

- Mash 1 cup beans together with 1 cup broth until smooth.

- Place bean mixture with remaining broth and beans, chicken, onion, corn, chiles and spices in Dutch oven or large cook pot.

- Mix thoroughly. Bring to boil, cover, reduce heat and simmer 40 to 60 minutes. Do not over cook.

- To serve, ladle into bowls and top with salsa and sour cream.

Yield: 10 cups

Serve with red tortilla chips for a festive and colorful Christmas Eve supper.

Chili Con Carne

1	pound ground beef	¼	teaspoon crushed pepper
1	large onion, minced	1	bay leaf
1	clove garlic, minced	1	tablespoon chili powder
1	(16-ounce) can tomatoes, chopped and not drained	¼	cup fresh basil or 1 teaspoon dried basil
1	(6-ounce) can tomato paste	1½	teaspoons salt
½	teaspoon celery salt	1	(16-ounce) can pinto beans, drained
½	teaspoon caraway seeds		

- Sauté beef, onion and garlic in heavy saucepan until browned.
- Add chopped tomatoes, tomato sauce and seasonings. Simmer 1 hour.
- Add beans and simmer 30 minutes more.

Yield: 4 servings

Glenda's Daddy's Chili

2	pounds ground beef	1	(14-ounce) bottle ketchup
1	stick butter or margarine	4	(14-ounce) cans diced tomatoes
2	green peppers, chopped		Red pepper and garlic powder
2	onions, chopped		to taste
1	cup chopped celery	3	(14-ounce) cans light red
¼	cup chili powder		kidney beans
1	(12-ounce) bottle chili sauce		

- Brown beef in skillet; drain and set aside.
- Sauté green pepper, onion and celery in butter in a Dutch oven.
- Add beef and all other ingredients except beans. Simmer 1 to 1½ hours.
- Add beans and cook 30 minutes longer.

Yield: 10 servings

Golden Soup

1 ounce butter	1 cup whipping cream
1 medium onion, finely chopped	Salt and pepper
1 pound carrots, peeled and sliced	Grated nutmeg
2½ cups chicken stock	Snipped chives
1½ cups fresh orange juice	

- Melt butter in large saucepan. Add onions and carrots and sauté on low heat until vegetables are soft.
- Add chicken stock and cook until vegetables fall apart when pierced.
- Remove from heat and let cool. Puree in food processor.
- Return to low heat and add orange juice and cream.
- Add salt and pepper to taste.
- Serve hot or cold and garnish with nutmeg and chives.

Yield: 6 to 8 servings

Homemade Vegetable Soup

1 soup bone, flat with meat	6 carrots, chopped
1 (28-ounce) can tomatoes	1 (15-ounce) can green beans
1 (6-ounce) can tomato paste	½-1 cup shredded cabbage
4 cups water	5-6 sprigs parsley
4 stalks (ribs) celery, chopped	⅔ cup small elbow macaroni
4 onions, chopped	Several sprigs thyme
1 (10-ounce) package frozen peas	Salt and pepper to taste

- Place soup bone in a large pot with lid. Cover with tomatoes and tomato paste.
- Add water and bring to boil. Reduce heat to low and cook 1 hour.
- Add vegetables and cook 30 minutes.
- Add macaroni and herbs and cook 30 more minutes. Season to taste.

Yield: 6 to 8 servings

The longer it cooks the better!

Ann's Green Vegetable Soup

1	bunch broccoli	1	teaspoon instant beef bouillon
1½	cups water	1	package Knorr Swiss Leek soup
4	green onions, chopped		mix
1	(10-ounce) package frozen	1	cup sour cream
	chopped spinach	1	tablespoon parsley

- Chop and cook broccoli including stems in 1½ cups water until tender; drain, reserving liquid.
- Put cooked broccoli through food processor and place in soup pot.
- Cook green onions and spinach in reserved liquid until tender; drain, reserving liquid.
- Put these vegetables through food processor and into soup pot.
- Add water to the remaining liquid to make 3 cups and add to pot.
- Add beef bouillon, Knorr soup mix and sour cream.
- Season to taste and heat to blend flavors. Sprinkle parsley on each serving.

Yield: 6 servings

A variety of green vegetables may be used: asparagus, peas and green beans in variable amounts; fresh, frozen, or left over.

"On A Roll Gourmet Deli"
Onion Soup

5	pounds onions, sliced ½-inch thick, then quartered
¼	pound butter
¾	cup flour
2	tablespoons paprika
2	teaspoons salt
1½	teaspoons pepper
3	quarts beef stock
1	bay leaf
	Sliced toasted French bread or croutons
	Sliced Swiss or provolone cheese

- Sauté onions in butter in heavy soup pot.
- Reduce heat to medium and cook for 1 hour, stirring occasionally.
- When onions are caramelized, add flour and cook for 15 minutes until flour taste is cooked out.
- Add rest of the ingredients and bring to a boil.
- Reduce heat to simmer and simmer covered for 3 hours.
- Remove from heat and cool. Refrigerate overnight for best results.
- Before serving, reheat soup and put in individual serving bowls. Top with toasted sliced French bread or croutons. Then top with slice of cheese, being sure the slice of cheese overlaps the rim of bowl. Heat until the cheese melts under a broiler or in a microwave.

Yield: 20 servings

Crock Pot Crowder Chowder

1½ cups dry crowder or field peas
1   ring smoked sausage, sliced in
     ½-inch rounds
1   onion, sliced
½   cup chopped celery tops
5   carrots, sliced
6-8 new potatoes, peeled and
     quartered

1   clove garlic, crushed
4-6 cups water
2   beef bouillon cubes
½   head of cabbage, sliced
1   tablespoon mustard
     Salt and pepper to taste

- Rinse and soak peas overnight.
- Precook sausage in microwave to remove fat.
- Place all other ingredients except cabbage, mustard, salt and pepper in crock pot.
- Cook on low 8 to 10 hours. Add cabbage and cook 1 hour on HIGH.
- Stir in mustard, salt and pepper.

Yield: 10 to 12 servings

Cold Cucumber-Shrimp Soup

2   large cucumbers, peeled,
     seeded and diced
     Salt
3   cups plain yogurt
1   cup whipping cream

1   cup chicken broth
1   cup tomato juice
2   cloves garlic, crushed
½   pound shrimp, cooked, peeled
     and diced

- Place cucumbers on paper towel and sprinkle generously with salt.
- Let stand for 30 minutes.
- Rinse cucumber thoroughly and drain; chop finely.
- Mix all remaining ingredients with cucumber and refrigerate at least 2 hours.
- Tastes better the longer it sits.

Yield: 8 servings

Captain Christian's Gazpacho

1½ cups chopped cucumbers,
 peeled and seeded
Salt
1 (48-ounce) can tomato juice
6 tomatoes, peeled, seeded and
 chopped
½ clove garlic, chopped

1 cup chopped green pepper
1 cup chopped onions
1 tablespoon olive oil
1 tablespoon parsley
1 teaspoon salt
½ cup wine vinegar

- Place chopped cucumbers on paper towels and sprinkle with enough salt to cover (this keeps them crunchy). Drain on paper towels for 30 minutes.
- Rinse cucumbers with cold water.
- Combine all ingredients in large bowl.
- Cover and refrigerate for at least 6 hours.

Yield: 6 to 8 servings

This keeps for several days and tastes better each day.

Cold Strawberry Soup

16 ounces strawberries
 (fresh or frozen)
1 cup sour cream

1 cup half-and-half
¼ cup sugar
¼ cup white wine

- Put all ingredients in food processor or blender. Process and chill.

Yield: 4 cups

Salads

Beaufort Harbor - *Watercolor*

Doris King

Mrs. King, a native of South Carolina, has lived in Beaufort since the 1950's and is a member of St. Paul's. She always enjoyed art, but only began studying and painting as an adult after years as a busy working wife and mother.

Strawberry Salad

2	(3-ounce) packages strawberry gelatin	1	cup crushed pineapple, undrained
1⅔	cups boiling water	2	ripe bananas, finely diced
2	(10-ounce) packages frozen strawberries	1	cup chopped pecans or walnuts
		1	pint sour cream

- Dissolve gelatin in boiling water.
- Add strawberries and stir to melt.
- Add pineapple, bananas and nuts.
- Pour ½ mixture into 9 x 13-inch glass dish.
- Refrigerate until firm, about 90 minutes. Do not refrigerate remaining gelatin mixture.
- Spread sour cream over firm mixture. Carefully pour remaining mixture over top of sour cream layer.
- Refrigerate until firm. Cut into squares and serve on lettuce.

Yield: 10 to 12 servings

Spicy Peach Salad

1	(3-ounce) package peach gelatin	2	tablespoons vinegar
¼	teaspoon cinnamon	1	cup diced canned peaches, drained - save syrup
⅛	teaspoon ground cloves		
1	cup boiling water	¾	cup peach syrup, add water if not ¾ cup
¼	cup sugar		

- Mix gelatin with spices. Dissolve in water.
- Add sugar, vinegar and peach syrup.
- Chill until slightly thickened; add peaches.
- Pour into 3-cup mold. Chill until firm.

Yield: 6 servings

Raspberry Salad

A festive dish for the holidays.

2 (3-ounce) packages raspberry gelatin	2 cups chopped pecans
2 cups boiling water	1 pint sour cream
2 (10-ounce) packages frozen raspberries	2 cups marshmallow, cut into small pieces (do not use miniature)
2 cups applesauce	

- Dissolve gelatin in water.

- Add berries, applesauce and pecans. Pour into a 9 x 13-inch glass or ceramic dish. Chill until firm.

- Mix sour cream and marshmallows. Refrigerate while salad is congealing.

- Spread evenly over salad. Serve on lettuce.

Yield: 10 to 12 servings

Cranberry Salad

2 cups fresh cranberries	1 envelope plain gelatin
1 cup sugar	⅓ cup water
⅔ cup orange juice	1 cup diced unpeeled apples
3 tablespoons lemon juice	1 cup chopped celery
1½ cups water	1 cup chopped pecans
1 (3-ounce) package lemon gelatin	

- Place first 5 ingredients in covered saucepan and cook together until cranberries pop open.

- Remove from stove and add lemon gelatin to mixture.

- Dissolve plain gelatin in ⅓ cup water and add to above mixture.

- Cool until slightly thickened.

- Add apples, celery and pecans.

- Pour into individual molds and refrigerate.

Yield: 12 servings

Bing Cherry Salad

1	(3-ounce) package black cherry gelatin	¼	cup cherry juice
1	(15-ounce) can Bing or dark cherries, pitted and halved, drained - save juice	½	cup pecan pieces
		½	cup mayonnaise
		½	cup sour cream
¾	cup white wine	⅛	cup cinnamon and sugar mixture

- Prepare gelatin as directed, using hot water to dissolve and white wine and cherry juice in place of cold water.
- Pour into 3-cup mold and refrigerate.
- Let thicken, then add cherries and nuts.
- When firmly set, mix mayonnaise and sour cream and spread over gelatin mixture.
- Sprinkle with cinnamon and sugar.

Yield: 6 servings

Goes well with red meat or poultry.

Pineapple and Cottage Cheese Salad

3½	cups crushed pineapple	1	(3-ounce) package lime gelatin
1	teaspoon salt	1	cup cottage cheese
1	(3-ounce) package lemon gelatin	1	cup mayonnaise
		½	cup chopped pecans

- Drain pineapple and save juice.
- Add water to juice to make 2 cups.
- Heat liquid to boiling and add salt and gelatins. Stir until dissolved.
- Cool to lukewarm and add remaining ingredients. Mix well.
- Pour into 9 x 13-inch pan or mold. Refrigerate until congealed.

Yield: 12 servings

Heavenly Orange Salad

2	cups boiling water	2	(11-ounce) cans Mandarin
2	(3-ounce) packages orange		oranges, drained
	gelatin	1	(3-ounce) package instant
1	(6-ounce) can frozen orange		lemon pudding
	juice, undiluted	1	cup milk
1	(15-ounce) can crushed	½	pint whipping cream, whipped
	pineapple, undrained		or 8-ounce whipped topping

- Mix water and gelatin, stir until dissolved.
- Stir in orange juice and cool.
- Add pineapple and oranges to gelatin mixture.
- Pour into 9 x 13-inch dish and refrigerate until congealed.
- Beat pudding mix with milk until slightly firm.
- Fold whipped cream or topping into pudding.
- Spread on top of firm gelatin. Chill until served.
- Cut into squares and serve on lettuce.

Yield: 12 servings

Served at ECW Fall Bazaar luncheons.

Congealed Fruit Salad

1	(3-ounce) package lemon gelatin	1	(11-ounce) can Mandarin oranges, undrained
2	(3-ounce) packages orange gelatin	¼	cup sugar
2	cups boiling water	1	tablespoon lemon rind
1	(15-ounce) can crushed pineapple, undrained	¼	cup lemon juice
2	(12-ounce) cans apricot nectar	2	eggs, beaten
		1	(8-ounce) container whipped topping
		1	cup grated sharp Cheddar cheese

- Dissolve gelatins in boiling water.
- Add pineapple, apricot nectar and oranges; stir.
- Pour into 9 x 13-inch dish or individual molds and congeal.
- Mix sugar, lemon rind, lemon juice and eggs in top of double boiler and cook until thickened.
- Remove from heat and cool. Add whipped topping and blend. Refrigerate.
- When salad is firm, spread dressing on top and sprinkle with cheese. Cut into squares and serve on lettuce leaves.

Yield: 12 to 15 servings

Ambrosia Salad Mold

1 (14-ounce) can pineapple chunks, undrained	6 ounces cream cheese, softened
1 envelope plain gelatin	1 (11-ounce) can Mandarin oranges
½ cup cold water	½ cup chopped pecans
Sugar to taste	½ cup coconut
Juice of 1 lemon	

- Drain pineapple. Add enough water to juice to equal 1 cup. Heat to boiling.
- Dissolve gelatin in the ½ cup cold water.
- Add gelatin to hot juice. Add sugar, lemon juice and cream cheese.
- Beat with wire whisk.
- Pour into 8 x 11-inch pan or mold. Refrigerate until semi-congealed.
- Add fruits, coconut and nuts. Chill until firm, about 1 to 1½ hours.

Yield: 8 to 10 servings

Mother's Frozen Fruit Salad

1 (8-ounce) package cream cheese	1 (4-ounce) jar maraschino cherries, drained and cut up
1 cup mayonnaise	
1 cup heavy cream, whipped	½-1 cup chopped pecans
1 (20-ounce) can fruit cocktail, drained	2 cups miniature marshmallows (optional)
1 (20-ounce) can crushed pineapple, drained	

- Soften cream cheese and beat with mayonnaise until smooth.
- Fold in whipped cream.
- Add fruits, nuts and marshmallows and blend well.
- Pour into individual molds or 9 x 13-inch freezer tray and freeze.
- Serve on lettuce.

Yield: 12 servings

Ribbon Salad

2	cups whole milk	1	(3-ounce) package lime gelatin
1	cup granulated sugar	1	(3-ounce) package orange gelatin
2	envelopes unflavored gelatin	1	(3-ounce) package lemon gelatin
½	cup cold water	1	(3-ounce) package red gelatin-
2	cups sour cream		cherry, strawberry or
1	teaspoon vanilla		raspberry

- Bring milk to boil; remove from heat; add sugar; cool to lukewarm.
- Dissolve unflavored gelatin in ½ cup cold water; add to milk mixture.
- Add sour cream and vanilla to milk mixture, whisk or blend until smooth.
- 1st Layer: Dissolve lime gelatin in ¾ cup boiling water, add ¾ cup ice cold water. Pour into 13 x 9-inch glass dish. Chill 45 minutes.
- 2nd layer: Slowly pour 1½ cup milk mixture over lime layer. Chill 30 minutes.
- 3rd Layer: Dissolve orange gelatin in ¾ cup boiling water, add ¾ cup ice cold water; slowly pour over milk layer. Chill 30 minutes.
- 4th Layer: Slowly pour 1½ cups milk mixture over orange layer. Chill 30 minutes.
- 5th Layer: Dissolve lemon gelatin in ¾ cup boiling water, add ¾ cup ice cold water; slowly pour over milk layer. Chill 30 minutes.
- 6th Layer: Slowly pour remainder of milk mixture over lemon layer. Chill 30 minutes.
- 7th Layer: Dissolve red gelatin in ¾ cups boiling water, add ¾ cups ice cold water, slowly pour over milk layer. Chill 30 minutes or until completely congealed.

Yield: 12 servings

Allow 4 hours to mix and layer salad. For a colorful holiday salad, use red and green gelatins alternately.

Fresh Fruit Salad with Yogurt Dressing

1	(20-ounce) can pineapple chunks, undrained	1	peach or 1 (15-ounce) can cling peaches, drained
1	red apple	1	nectarine
1	green apple	⅓	pound red and green grapes
1	yellow apple	2	bananas
1	green pear	2	cartons low calorie peach yogurt

- Place pineapple in large deep bowl.
- Cut apples, pear and peaches into bite-size pieces and add to pineapple, stirring after each to coat with juice.
- Cut grapes in half and add to above mixture.
- Let stand for 1 hour.
- Just before serving, slice bananas and stir into mixture, coating well with juice.
- Drain off pineapple juice. Add yogurt and stir well to coat fruit.
- Serve on lettuce or buffet style. Can sprinkle with nutmeg.

Yield: 12 to 15 servings

Texas Slaw

½	cup sugar	8	cups shredded cabbage
½	cup vinegar	1	cup sliced green pepper
¼	cup oil	1	carrot, coarsely shredded
1	cup thinly sliced red pepper		Salt and pepper to taste
1	medium onion, sliced thin		

- Whisk sugar, vinegar and oil together in large bowl.
- Add remaining ingredients and toss to combine.
- Season with salt and pepper to taste.
- Cover tightly and refrigerate for 4 hours, tossing occasionally.

Yield: 8 to 10 servings

Oriental Slaw

2	(3-ounce) packages ramen noodles (minus flavor packs)	½	teaspoon salt
		3	tablespoons soy sauce
¾	cup slivered almonds	¾	cup sugar
¾	stick butter	½	cup red wine vinegar
½	cup sunflower seeds or sesame seeds	1	head Napa or Chinese cabbage, torn into pieces
1	cup salad oil	5	green onions, chopped

- Break ramen noodles into pieces.
- Brown noodles and almonds in butter. Cool and add seeds.
- Mix oil, salt, soy sauce, sugar and vinegar in jar or bottle and shake well.
- Combine cabbage and onions in large bowl. Add noodle mixture and dressing and mix well.
- Serve immediately or can be refrigerated 2 to 3 hours.

Yield: 6 to 8 servings

"G & R Supermarket" Marinated Salad

4	cucumbers	6	tomatoes
3	bell peppers	1	(8-ounce) bottle Italian dressing
1	large onion		Salt and pepper to taste

- Cut vegetables into bite-size pieces.
- Pour dressing over vegetables and marinate in refrigerator.
- Keeps well in refrigerator for a week.

Yield: 8 to 10 servings

Crunchy Vegetable Salad

3	cups chopped fresh broccoli	¼	cup grated sharp Cheddar cheese
3	cups chopped fresh cauliflower	1	cup real mayonnaise
1	cup thinly sliced carrots	¼	cup sugar
¼	cup chopped onions	2	tablespoons cider vinegar
¼	cup real bacon bits		

- Mix first 6 ingredients in large bowl.
- Whisk mayonnaise, sugar and vinegar together for a dressing.
- Toss together salad and dressing until coated well.
- Refrigerate at least 2 hours before serving.

Yield: 12 servings

Served at 1999 ECW Fall Bazaar Luncheon.

Marinated Asparagus Salad

2	(14½-ounce) cans asparagus spears	1	stalk celery, finely chopped
½	green pepper, chopped	½	cup wine vinegar
½	red or yellow pepper, chopped	½	cup sugar
1	small bunch green onions and tops, chopped	¾	cup vegetable oil
		1	clove garlic
		½	teaspoon paprika

- Drain asparagus and place in container for marinating.
- Mix all remaining ingredients and pour over asparagus.
- Marinate 3 to 4 hours or overnight in refrigerator.
- Serve on lettuce.

Yield: 4 to 6 servings

Tart Asparagus Congealed Salad

1	(14½-ounce) can asparagus spears	¾	teaspoon white pepper
⅓	cup plus 1 tablespoon vinegar	1	cup chopped celery
1	(3-ounce) package lemon gelatin	1	cup chopped green onion
2	tablespoons lemon juice	1	can water chestnuts, drained and chopped fine
1	teaspoon Lawry's seasoned garlic salt (do not substitute)	¼	cup honey
		¾	cup mayonnaise
			Lettuce

- Drain asparagus and reserve liquid. Cut into 1-inch pieces.
- Combine asparagus juice and vinegar, add water to make 1 cup. Bring to a boil. Pour this over gelatin and stir to dissolve.
- Add lemon juice. Add salt, pepper, celery, onions and water chestnuts.
- Carefully fold in asparagus and pour into individual molds. Refrigerate overnight.
- Combine honey and mayonnaise. Blend thoroughly and spread on top of each mold. Serve on lettuce.

Yield: 6 servings

Broccoli and Almond Pasta Salad

6	tablespoons vegetable oil	¾	cup slivered almonds, toasted
1	teaspoon sesame oil	8	ounces penne, seashells or elbow pasta, cooked and cooled
¼	cup vinegar		
1	clove garlic, minced		
1	bunch broccoli, florets only, steamed	2	green onions, chopped
		½	cup Parmesan cheese

- Mix first 4 ingredients in a jar for dressing.
- Put next 4 ingredients in large bowl and pour dressing over all, tossing to mix.
- Add cheese to taste, stirring to mix.

Yield: 4 servings

Asparagus and Tomato Pasta Salad

2	cups diagonally sliced asparagus (about 1 pound)	⅛	teaspoon salt
1	cup uncooked small seashell pasta	¼	teaspoon freshly ground pepper
		1½	cups quartered cherry tomatoes
⅓	cup orange juice	1	cup diced yellow bell pepper
3	tablespoons white wine vinegar	⅓	cup chopped kalamata or black olives
2	tablespoons water	¼	cup thinly sliced green onions
1	tablespoon olive oil	2	tablespoons capers
2	teaspoons Dijon mustard	⅓	cup thinly sliced fresh basil

- Steam asparagus, covered, 2 minutes; drain and set aside.
- Cook seashell pasta as directed on package.
- Combine orange juice and next 6 ingredients in a large bowl; stir well with a wire whisk.
- Add asparagus, pasta and remaining ingredients; toss well.

Yield: 6 servings

Best when prepared ahead. Add basil 1 hour before serving if the salad is prepared well in advance of serving.

Broccoli-Raisin Salad

4-5	cups chopped broccoli	1	cup chopped celery
⅔	cup raisins	1	cup Miracle Whip
½	cup chopped almonds, peanuts, or sunflower seeds	½	cup sugar
		3	teaspoons vinegar
½	cup chopped onion		Salt and pepper to taste

- Toss all ingredients together and serve. May be refrigerated.

Yield: 8 to 10 servings

Broccoli-Mushroom Salad

1	bunch broccoli, chopped	½	cup raisins
5	hard-boiled eggs, chopped	½	cup chopped nuts (optional)
½	pound fresh mushrooms, sliced	¾	cup mayonnaise
1	onion, chopped	3	tablespoons tarragon vinegar
½	pound bacon, cooked and crumbled	3	tablespoons sugar
			Salt and pepper to taste

- Mix first 7 ingredients in a large bowl.
- Mix mayonnaise, vinegar and sugar and pour over salad 4 hours before serving.
- Add salt and pepper to taste. Refrigerate.

Yield: 8 to 10 servings

Portobello Salad

Portobello mushrooms - 1 per serving	Red pepper
Teriyaki sauce	Green pepper
Salad greens	Oil
Purple onion	Balsamic vinegar
	Grated Parmesan cheese

- Marinate mushrooms in teriyaki sauce overnight.
- Grill mushrooms and set aside.
- Arrange greens on each salad plate.
- Cut onion and peppers into ¼-inch slices and add to greens.
- Place mushroom on top of greens and vegetables.
- Sprinkle with oil and vinegar to taste; add cheese.

Yield: 1 or more

Cauliflower Salad

1	head cauliflower	1	package dry Italian dressing,
1	(8-ounce) jar salad olives,		prepared as directed
	drained	4	ounces blue cheese, crumbled

- Separate cauliflower into small pieces.
- Add olives and prepared dressing.
- Chill 2 hours or overnight.
- Just before serving, stir in blue cheese.

Yield: 6 to 8 servings

Kathryn W's Tomato Aspic

4	envelopes plain gelatin	5	tablespoons sugar
1½	cups cold water	½	cup apple cider vinegar
6	cups tomato juice	3	tablespoons onion juice
¾	teaspoon salt	1	teaspoon cayenne pepper

- Mix gelatin with water to soften.
- Heat 3 cups tomato juice to almost boiling.
- Add gelatin mixture and almost boil again.
- Add remaining juice and all other ingredients.
- Mix well and pour into oiled 2-quart mold or 9 x 13-inch casserole.
- Refrigerate to congeal. Best if prepared one day ahead.

Yield: 12 servings

Tomato Aspic

2	cups tomato juice
1	(3-ounce) package lemon gelatin
	Juice of 1 lemon
2	tablespoons vinegar
1	tablespoon Worcestershire sauce
½	teaspoon salt

- Chill 1 cup tomato juice.
- Heat remaining 1 cup tomato juice to almost boiling and dissolve gelatin in it.
- Add cold tomato juice and remaining ingredients; stir.
- Pour into individual molds and refrigerate until congealed

Yield: 6 to 8 servings

Cool Cucumber Salad

2	cups sliced carrots
2	cups sliced cucumbers
½	cup diced celery
1	onion, chopped
1	cup vinegar
1	teaspoon celery seed
1	teaspoon salt
1	teaspoon pepper
¾	cup sugar

- Mix all ingredients and marinate in refrigerator several hours.

Yield: 6 to 8 servings

Lettuce and Red Onion Salad

½-1 head lettuce, washed, dried and   1 pint mayonnaise
    torn into pieces   Parmesan cheese
2-3 medium red onions, thinly sliced

- Cover large platter with lettuce.
- Layer onion over lettuce to cover.
- Cover with mayonnaise. Sprinkle cheese over entire salad.
- Cover tightly with plastic wrap and refrigerate overnight.

Yield: 10 to 12 servings

Deerfield Special "Caesar" Salad

1-2 cloves garlic, minced   ⅓ cup olive oil
    Juice of ½ lemon   1 large bunch of romaine lettuce
1 teaspoon Worcestershire sauce   ⅓ cup grated Parmesan cheese
½ teaspoon salt   ¼ cup cooked and crumbled bacon
¼ teaspoon dry mustard   ½ cup croutons
    Pepper   Salt

- Make dressing of first 7 ingredients using blender or shaker bottle.
- Wash and drain lettuce and tear into bite-size pieces.
- Just before serving, pour dressing over greens.
- Add cheese, bacon and croutons. Season to taste.
- Toss and serve.

Yield: 6 servings

Wilted Spinach Salad with Spicy Scallops

1	large bunch spinach leaves, washed, dried and de-stemmed	½	pound scallops
		2	tablespoons sliced green onions
1	tablespoon dry sherry	1	teaspoon minced garlic
1	tablespoon rice vinegar	1	teaspoon minced gingerroot
	Salt and pepper to taste	⅛	teaspoon pepper flakes
3	tablespoons olive oil	2	teaspoons toasted sesame seeds

- Toss spinach with sherry, vinegar, salt and pepper in large bowl. Set aside.
- Heat oil in skillet and sauté scallops, onion, garlic, gingerroot and pepper flakes.
- Pour scallop mixture over spinach and toss just until combined and spinach wilts.
- Serve on individual salad plates and sprinkle with sesame seeds.

Yield: 4 to 6 servings

Winter Salad

1	head romaine lettuce, torn	2	ounces blue cheese, crumbled
½	head curly endive lettuce, torn	¼	cup walnuts, broken
1	can sliced beets, drained		Juice of 1 lemon
2	Granny Smith apples, cored and cubed	¼	cup olive oil
		½	teaspoon salt
1	bulb fennel, cored and thinly sliced		Pepper to taste

- Toss salad greens in a large bowl.
- Layer beets, apples and fennel, ending with cheese and nuts.
- Combine lemon juice, oil, salt and pepper.
- Pour over salad when ready to serve.

Yield: 8 servings

Makes a beautiful Christmas salad. Also nice served with a hearty soup.

Charity Ball Salad

2   (15-ounce) cans cut string beans
1   (14-ounce) can artichoke hearts
1   (8-ounce) can button mushrooms
1   (4-ounce) can sliced pimento
1   (7-ounce) can pitted black
     olives, drained and sliced
4   small white onions, cut into rings
1   cup vinegar
1   onion, diced
¾   teaspoon seasoned pepper
1   teaspoon garlic salt
2   tablespoons sugar
1   cup oil
1½ teaspoons seasoned salt
1   teaspoon Accent
1   teaspoon oregano

- Combine first 6 ingredients.
- Mix remaining ingredients and boil.
- Cool and pour over vegetables.
- Refrigerate overnight.

Yield: 8 to 10 servings

Black-Eyed Pea Salad

ECW Bazaar Luncheon hit!

1   (15-ounce) can black-eyed peas,
     rinsed and drained or ¾ cup
     dried peas, cooked and
     drained
1   (15-ounce) can whole kernel
     yellow corn, rinsed and
     drained
½   cup chopped green pepper
½   cup chopped red pepper
½   cup chopped onion
¼   cup oil
2   tablespoons water
½   cup sugar
½   cup vinegar

- Mix peas, corn, green and red pepper and onions in a bowl.
- Combine oil, water, sugar and vinegar in a separate bowl and mix.
- Pour marinade over vegetables and mix well.
- Refrigerate 4 to 8 hours before serving.

Yield: 6 to 8 servings

Three Bean Salad

1	(15-ounce) can green beans	1	green pepper, diced
1	(14-ounce) can kidney beans	1	cup vinegar
1	(15-ounce) can green peas	1	cup sugar
1	(2-ounce) jar diced pimento	½	cup vegetable oil
1	cup sliced celery	½	teaspoon salt
½	cup chopped onion	1	teaspoon paprika

- Drain and rinse beans, peas and pimento and toss with celery, onion and pepper.
- Mix vinegar, sugar, oil, salt and paprika well. Pour over vegetable mixture.
- Cover and marinate at least 12 hours in refrigerator.

Yield: 8 servings

Five Bean Salad

1	(15-ounce) can white shoe peg corn	1	(7-ounce) jar diced pimento
		2	stalks celery, chopped
1	(15-ounce) can butter beans	1	onion, chopped
1	(15-ounce) can crowder peas	½	cup canola oil
1	(15-ounce) can field peas	½	cup sugar
1	(15-ounce) can black-eyed peas	½	cup vinegar
1	(15-ounce) can small green peas		Salt and pepper to taste

- Drain and rinse canned items.
- Add celery and onion to canned vegetables and mix.
- Mix oil, sugar and vinegar and pour over above mixture. Season to taste.
- Refrigerate. Serve cold.

Yield: 12 to 15 servings

Blue Cheese Potato Salad

3	pounds red-skinned potatoes, cooked and cubed	¾	cup Miracle Whip
½	cup chopped onions	¼	cup sour cream
1	teaspoon garlic salt	4	ounces crumbled blue cheese
			Salt and pepper to taste

- Combine potatoes, onions and garlic salt. Toss gently.
- Stir together salad dressing, sour cream and blue cheese.
- Add to potato mixture. Season to taste and toss gently.
- Chill before serving.

Yield: 10 servings

Summer Potato Salad

6	medium potatoes, scrubbed, not peeled	1	tablespoon white wine vinegar
1	cup chopped onion	2	teaspoons Dijon mustard
⅔	cup low sodium chicken broth	1	teaspoon fresh ground pepper
½	cup olive oil	1	tablespoon fresh lemon juice
			Salt to taste

- Drop potatoes into boiling water, enough to cover completely.
- Boil until they show slight resistance when pierced.
- Drain, peel and cut into ¼-inch slices.
- Combine onions, broth, oil, vinegar, mustard and pepper in a saucepan.
- Boil over high heat. Reduce heat and simmer uncovered 5 minutes.
- Remove from heat and add lemon juice.
- Pour sauce over potatoes and coat evenly. Serve warm or at room temperature.

Yield: 4 to 6 servings

Optional additions: crumbled bacon, fresh dill.

Tuna Apple Salad

1	(6-ounce) can water packed tuna or ¾ cup fresh tuna	1	green onion, diced
¼-½ cup chopped celery		4-6	tablespoons mayonnaise
1	Granny Smith apple, unpeeled and diced	1	teaspoon lemon juice
			Salt and pepper
			Lettuce

- Drain tuna; mix with all other ingredients except lettuce.
- May use immediately or chill 1 to 2 hours.
- Serve on lettuce or as a sandwich.

Yield: 4 servings or 2 to 3 sandwiches

Buffalo Chicken Salad

2	pounds boneless, skinless chicken breasts	3-6	ounces Crystal Hot Sauce
3	ounces buttermilk	3-6	ounces mayonnaise
2	teaspoons brown sugar	3-6	ounces blue cheese, crumbled
1	ounce lemon juice	½	purple onion, julienned
3	ounces Crystal Hot Sauce (for Buffalo wings)	1	stalk celery, julienned
	Dash cayenne pepper, salt and pepper	1	teaspoon parsley
		16	ounces penne pasta, cooked

- Marinate chicken in buttermilk, brown sugar, lemon juice and hot sauce at least 1 hour, but better over night.
- Sprinkle chicken with cayenne, salt and pepper.
- Grill chicken and then cut into bite-size pieces.
- In a blender, blend hot sauce, mayonnaise and blue cheese.
- Combine cooked chicken, sauce, onion, celery, parsley and cooked pasta.
- Top with extra crumbled blue cheese. Refrigerate.

Yield: 6 to 8 servings

Chicken Salad Hugo

3 cups cooked diced chicken	½ cup toasted almonds
4 green onions, chopped	1 (5-ounce) can sliced water
1 cup mayonnaise	chestnuts
(Hellmann's recommended)	2 teaspoons curry powder
2 tablespoons chutney	Juice of 1 lemon
(London Pub Major Grey	Lettuce leaves
recommended)	

- Mix all ingredients except lettuce and toss well. Refrigerate.
- Serve on lettuce.

Yield: 4 to 6 servings

Southern Chicken Salad

4 cups diced cooked chicken	1 teaspoon dried parsley or
1½ cups chopped celery	2 teaspoons fresh parsley
1 tablespoon Durkee's special	1 teaspoon dill weed
sauce (optional)	Salt and pepper to taste
1 teaspoon lemon juice	Cayenne pepper (optional)
2 large eggs, boiled and chopped	½ cup mayonnaise
	½ cup sour cream

- Mix all ingredients except mayonnaise and sour cream.
- Add mayonnaise and sour cream to moisten; if more is needed, use equal amounts of each.
- Adjust seasonings of salt, pepper and cayenne to taste.

Yield: 8 servings

An ECW Bazaar luncheon favorite which can be easily increased to serve a crowd.

Shrimp and Seashells

½	cup water	1	tablespoon seasoning salt
½	cup cream sherry	1	cup seashell pasta, uncooked
1	pound fresh shrimp, peeled and thoroughly washed in several changes of cold water	1	cup chopped celery
		2	tablespoons grated onion
		½	cup mayonnaise

- Place water and sherry in 2-quart saucepan and bring to a boil.
- Add shrimp and seasoning salt and boil gently 2 minutes; remove from heat and let sit in water for 5 minutes.
- Remove shrimp with slotted spoon, reserving liquid, and place shrimp in a large bowl to cool.
- Add seashell pasta to boiling shrimp liquid, cooking for 5 minutes or until done.
- Cut cooled shrimp into bite-size pieces while pasta cooks.
- Drain pasta, place in bowl with shrimp, cool.
- Add celery, onion and mayonnaise and toss to coat. Refrigerate.

Yield: 4 servings

Optional additions include chopped bell pepper, chopped hard-boiled eggs, or chives.

Bayley's West Indies Salad

1	medium onion, thinly sliced	4	ounces vegetable oil
1	pound fresh white lump crabmeat	3	ounces cider vinegar
	Salt and pepper to taste	4	ounces ice water

- Place a layer of onion in bottom of 1-quart ceramic bowl.
- Add layer of crabmeat, then salt and pepper to taste.
- Continue layering until crabmeat is used.
- Pour oil over crabmeat, then vinegar and then water.
- Cover and refrigerate several hours. Toss before serving.
- Serve on lettuce or as an appetizer with crackers.

Yield: 4 to 6 servings

Crab Salad

1	pound fresh or imitation crabmeat	4	tablespoons plain yogurt
¼	cup chopped onion	2	tablespoons salad dressing (either mayonnaise-type or Italian)
¼	cup chopped green pepper		
¼	cup chopped celery		Paprika and salt to taste
1	tablespoon prepared mustard		

- Mix all ingredients and refrigerate for 1 hour.

Yield: 4 to 6 servings

Vegetables and
Side Dishes

Lisa Stockard '94

New Life - Watercolor

Lisa Stockard

Mrs. Stockard, a self-taught watercolorist, has been painting for over ten years. A native of Greensboro, N.C., she lived in Beaufort where her husband, Matthew, was rector of St. Paul's. They now reside in Greenville, N.C. with their dog, Dylan. She directs a church youth choir and continues to paint.

Asparagus Casserole

1	stick butter or margarine	1	cup grated sharp Cheddar cheese
1½	cups crushed Ritz crackers, divided	2-3	(15-ounce) cans long asparagus spears
4	tablespoons butter	2-3	hard-boiled eggs, sliced
3	tablespoons flour	1	(2-ounce) jar pimento, drained
1½	cups milk	½	cup slivered almonds
	Pinch salt and cayenne pepper		

- Melt butter in 9 x 13-inch dish and mix in 1 cup cracker crumbs.
- In a saucepan, melt butter and add flour, mixing until smooth.
- Add milk, pepper, salt and heat until slightly thickened.
- Add cheese, stirring until smooth.
- Place drained asparagus over the crumb mixture.
- Add boiled eggs and pimento.
- Pour sauce over all and sprinkle with almonds and remaining cracker crumbs.
- Bake at 350° for 30 minutes or until bubbly around sides.

Yield: 6 to 8 servings

Steamed Asparagus
with Garlic Ginger Sauce

2	pounds asparagus	1	teaspoon Asian sesame oil
2	teaspoons cornstarch	1	tablespoon vegetable oil
½	cup water	2	tablespoons minced, peeled
2	tablespoons soy sauce		fresh gingerroot
1	tablespoon medium dry sherry	1½	tablespoons minced garlic
	or scotch	2	tablespoons sesame seeds,
1	teaspoon sugar		lightly toasted
½	teaspoon salt		

- In a steamer set over boiling water, steam asparagus, covered, until just crisp-tender, about 2 to 3 minutes.

- Transfer asparagus to a colander and rinse under cold water to stop cooking.

- Drain well. Cut in 2-inch pieces for easier stir-frying.

- In a 1 cup measure, stir together cornstarch and water until dissolved.

- Stir in soy sauce, sherry or scotch, sugar, salt and sesame oil.

- Heat wok or heavy skillet over high heat until hot and add vegetable oil.

- Heat vegetable oil until hot but not smoking and stir-fry gingerroot and garlic 30 seconds.

- Add asparagus and stir-fry 30 seconds.

- Stir cornstarch mixture and add to asparagus.

- Bring liquid to a boil, stirring and stir-fry until asparagus is well coated.

- Remove from heat.

- Sprinkle asparagus with sesame seeds and toss.

Yield: 6 servings

Vegetable Trio

2	tablespoons butter	1	(4-ounce) can mushrooms
2	tablespoons all-purpose flour	1	(14-ounce) can artichokes
2	tablespoons asparagus juice	1	(2½-ounce) package sliced
1	cup heavy cream		almonds
¾	pound sharp Cheddar cheese shredded	2	eggs, hard-boiled and sliced
			Salt and pepper to taste
2	(15-ounce) cans asparagus - save juice		Paprika

- Preheat oven to 350°.
- Make white sauce with butter, flour, asparagus juice and cream.
- Add cheese and stir until melted, set sauce aside.
- Combine asparagus, mushrooms, artichokes, almonds and eggs.
- Add salt and pepper to taste.
- Put ½ of vegetable mixture into a greased 2-quart casserole.
- Cover with ½ of the sauce. Repeat layers of vegetables and sauce.
- Sprinkle top with paprika.
- Bake for 30 minutes or until hot and bubbly.

Yield: 6 to 8 servings

Broccoli Casserole

2	(10-ounce) packages frozen chopped broccoli or broccoli florets	1	egg, beaten
½	stick butter or margarine	1	cup grated sharp Cheddar cheese
1	onion, chopped		Salt and pepper to taste
¼	cup flour	1	(5-ounce) can water chestnuts (optional)
1	(10¾-ounce) can cream of mushroom soup	1	stack Ritz crackers, crushed or 2 cups herb stuffing mix
1	cup mayonnaise	½	stick butter, melted

- Cook broccoli according to package directions and drain thoroughly.
- Sauté onions in butter, then add flour and blend well.
- Mix soup, mayonnaise, egg, cheese, broccoli, salt and pepper and water chestnuts, if desired. Blend in onions.
- Pour into greased 9 x 13-inch baking dish and bake at 350° for 30 minutes.
- Top with buttered crumbs and bake 15 to 20 minutes or until brown and bubbly.

Yield: 10 to 12 servings

Lenoxville Baked Beans

1	(16-ounce) can pork and beans	1	medium onion, chopped
2	tablespoons brown sugar	4	strips bacon, cut into 1-inch pieces
¼	teaspoon dry mustard		
¼	cup ketchup		

- Combine all ingredients except bacon.
- Bake in greased covered casserole at 350° for 20 minutes.
- Uncover and top with 4 strips of bacon.
- Continue baking 20 minutes.

Yield: 4 to 6 servings

Bern's Baked Beans

4 tablespoons bacon drippings
2 cups chopped onions
3 buds garlic, crushed
1 (53-ounce) can pork and beans, drained
1 (15½-ounce) can kidney beans, drained
1 (8½-ounce) can baby lima beans, drained
½ cup brown sugar
¼ cup vinegar
½ teaspoon pepper
1 teaspoon salt
1 teaspoon prepared mustard
½ cup ketchup

- Brown onions in bacon drippings.
- Mix all other ingredients together with onions.
- Bake in 9 x 13-inch covered casserole at 350° for 45 minutes.
- Remove cover, stir and bake uncovered an additional 10 minutes.

Yield: 12 servings

German Green Beans

2 cups fresh green beans
1 strip bacon
¼ cup chopped onion
1 teaspoon flour
¼ cup vinegar
½ cup water
2 tablespoons sugar or sugar replacement

- Cook green beans in boiling water until tender and drain.
- Cut bacon into ½-inch pieces; place in skillet and add onion.
- Sauté until bacon is crisp and onion is tender; drain.
- Blend flour, vinegar, water and sugar in a jar or blender.
- In skillet, add jar mixture to bacon and onions.
- Cook over low heat to thicken slightly.
- Add green beans and heat until warm.

Yield: 4 servings

Deviled Brussels Sprouts

1   pound fresh Brussels sprouts
⅔   cup butter, melted
2   tablespoons prepared mustard
1   teaspoon Worcestershire sauce

½   teaspoon salt
¼   teaspoon crushed red pepper or
     cayenne pepper

- Wash sprouts, cut off stem ends and slash bottom end with a X.
- Place sprouts in small amount of boiling water, cover and simmer 7 minutes or until tender.
- Drain, place in serving dish.
- Combine remaining ingredients and pour over sprouts.

Yield: 6 servings

Oakwood Acres Collard Casserole

4   cups cooked and chopped
     collards
1   (10¾-ounce) can cream of
     mushroom soup
1   medium onion, chopped
1   cup mayonnaise
2   eggs, beaten

1   (5-ounce) can sliced water
     chestnuts, drained
1   cup grated sharp Cheddar
     cheese
Salt and pepper to taste
24 Ritz crackers, crumbled
Butter

- Mix all ingredients, except crackers and butter.
- Place in 9 x 13-inch baking dish. Spread crackers on top and dot with butter.
- Bake at 350° for 30 minutes.

Yield: 10 to 12 servings

Red Cabbage with Apples

1	(2 to 2½ pound) red cabbage	½	cup chopped onion
⅔	cup red wine vinegar	1	whole onion, pierced with
2	tablespoons sugar		2 whole cloves
2	tablespoons bacon fat	1	small bay leaf
2	medium cooking apples,	5	cups boiling water
	peeled, cored and cut into	3	tablespoons red wine
	⅛-inch thick slices	3	tablespoons red currant jelly

- Wash cabbage and cut into quarters. Remove core and shred into ⅛-inch wide slices.
- Place cabbage in large bowl, sprinkle with vinegar and sugar. Toss to coat evenly.
- In a heavy 4 to 5-quart saucepan, melt bacon fat over moderate heat.
- Add the apples and chopped onions. Cook, stirring frequently for 5 minutes.
- Add the cabbage, whole onion with cloves and the bay leaf; stir thoroughly and pour in the boiling water.
- Bring to boil, stirring occasionally and reduce heat to lowest point.
- Cover and simmer 1½ to 2 hours or until cabbage is tender.
- Check from time to time to make sure cabbage is moist. If not, add a little boiling water.
- Just before serving, remove the whole onion and bay leaf and stir in wine and currant jelly.

Yield: 10 to 12 servings

Shell Landing Corn Pudding

1	egg, beaten	1-2	teaspoons salt
½	cup milk	1	(14¾-ounce) can creamed corn
2	tablespoons sugar	1	(15¼-ounce) whole kernel corn,
1	tablespoon flour		drained
4	tablespoons butter, melted		

- Mix egg, milk, sugar, flour, butter and salt.
- Add corn to mixture and blend well.
- Bake in a greased 2-quart baking dish at 350° for 1 hour.

Yield: 6 servings

Scalloped Eggplant

1	medium eggplant, peeled and cut into ¼-inch slices		Salt and pepper to taste
		½	cup grated sharp Cheddar cheese
2	slices bread, crust removed and torn into pieces	¼	cup Parmesan cheese
			Cracker crumbs
1	cup milk		Butter
1	egg, beaten		

- Cook peeled eggplant in salted water until tender, about 15 minutes.
- Drain and mash.
- Put bread in 8 x 8-inch baking dish.
- Mix milk and egg. Beat until foamy.
- Add eggplant, salt and pepper to egg mixture and beat with a fork.
- Fold in cheeses and pour over bread.
- Top with cracker crumbs and dot with butter.
- Bake at 350° for 45 minutes.

Yield: 4 to 6 servings

Mushroom Rice

½	cup margarine	2	tablespoons sherry
1	cup uncooked rice	¼	teaspoon salt
2	(4-ounce) cans sliced	⅛	teaspoon garlic powder
	mushrooms, undrained	⅛	teaspoon pepper
1	(10½-ounce) can beef broth		

- Melt margarine in a 1½-quart baking dish.
- Add all other ingredients and stir.
- Bake covered at 350° for 1 hour or until liquid is absorbed.

Yield: 6 servings

Balsamic Roasted Onions

4	large red onions (2 pounds)	½	teaspoon salt
1	tablespoon olive oil	1	tablespoon mixed dried herbs
⅓	cup balsamic vinegar		or ¼ cup fresh herbs

- Preheat oven to 450°.
- Slice tops off onions and peel, leaving root ends. Cut each onion into 8 wedges taking care that wedges stay intact.
- Place onions in a single layer in a 9 x 13-inch baking dish and toss gently with oil.
- Replace in single layer. Pour vinegar over onions and sprinkle with salt and herbs.
- Cover with foil and bake for 45 minutes.
- Uncover and bake for 5 to 10 minutes until onions are soft and caramelized on bottom.

Yield: 4 servings

Suggested herbs include tarragon, marjoram and basil.

Onion Casserole (Soubise)

15 cups chopped Spanish onions	1½ cups grated Swiss cheese
8 tablespoons butter	1½ cups half-and-half or whipping
2 cups rice	cream
6 cups water, salted	¼ teaspoon nutmeg

- Sauté onions in butter until limp.
- Cook rice in water for 5 minutes. Drain well.
- Mix rice, onions, cheese, cream and nutmeg.
- Bake uncovered in a 9 x 13-inch baking dish for 1 hour at 325°.

Yield: 8 to 10 servings

Can be frozen. Good holiday side dish with beef or turkey.

Squash, Corn and Onion Combo

4 slices bacon, fried crisp and drained	1-1½ cups fresh or frozen corn or 1 (15-ounce) can whole kernel corn, drained
4-5 small yellow squash	1 teaspoon salt
2 small - medium onions	½ teaspoon pepper

- Fry bacon slices in large skillet, drain, set aside.
- Slice squash and onions in round.
- Fry over medium high in bacon drippings until onions brown slightly.
- Add corn, salt and pepper. Stir to mix.
- Cover and continue cooking 15 minutes, stirring occasionally.
- Mound in a bowl and crumble crisp bacon over all.

Yield: 6 servings

Martini Sauerkraut

2	quarts water	1	bay leaf
½	pound bacon	2	cups canned beef broth
¼	cup butter or margarine	1	cup dry vermouth
1	cup sliced onions	¼	cup gin
½	cup sliced carrot		Salt and pepper to taste
2	(14-ounce) cans sauerkraut, drained		

- Boil water in large Dutch oven.
- Add bacon, reduce heat and simmer 10 minutes.
- Drain; chop bacon, set aside.
- Melt butter in Dutch oven and add chopped bacon, onion and carrots.
- Cook over low heat for 10 minutes.
- Stir in sauerkraut. Cover and simmer 10 minutes.
- Bury bay leaf in sauerkraut mixture and pour beef broth, vermouth and gin over all.
- Season with salt and pepper, stirring to mix.
- Cover and bake at 325° for 4 hours or until liquid is absorbed.
- Remove bay leaf before serving.

Yield: 6 to 8 servings

Butternut Squash Risotto

1	small butternut squash (about 1½ pounds)	3	tablespoons unsalted butter
1¾	cups chicken broth	½	cup long grain rice (not instant)
½	cup water	¼	cup dry white wine
1	small onion, chopped	1	tablespoon chopped chives
1	large garlic clove, sliced thin		Salt and pepper to taste
1¼	teaspoons minced peeled fresh gingerroot		Parmesan cheese

- Preheat oven at 450°.
- Half squash and discard seeds. Peel 1 half and dice.
- Put other half, cut side down in greased shallow baking pan, surround with diced squash and season with salt and pepper.
- Bake squash in middle of oven stirring diced half occasionally until tender and lightly brown (about 15 to 20 minutes).
- Scoop out flesh and coarsely chop.
- Bring water and broth to a simmer in a saucepan. Keep hot.
- Cook onion, garlic and gingerroot in butter in another saucepan over low heat until softened.
- Stir in rice and cook for 1 minute over moderate heat while stirring.
- Add wine and cook until absorbed.
- Add ¼ cup broth and water mixture until absorbed.
- Continue adding broth, stirring constantly until each addition has been absorbed and about half the broth has been used.
- Stir in diced and chopped squash in the same manner.
- Continue cooking until the rice is tender and creamy looking.
- Stir in chives and salt and pepper to taste.
- Garnish with chives and Parmesan cheese.

Yield: 4 servings

May be made ahead and warmed in baking dish.

Summer Squash Casserole

An old reliable summer favorite!

2   pounds yellow squash, sliced -
     about 6 cups
1½ cups chopped onion
1   (10½-ounce) can cream of
     chicken soup
1   cup sour cream
1   cup grated carrot

1   (2-ounce) jar pimento, drained
     (optional)
1   (5-ounce) can sliced water
     chestnuts (optional)
     Salt and pepper to taste
1   (8-ounce) package herb
     seasoned stuffing
½   cup margarine, melted

- Cook squash and onion in water to cover until tender; drain thoroughly.

- Combine soup, sour cream, carrots, pimentos, water chestnuts, salt and pepper.

- Fold in squash and onions.

- Mix stuffing and margarine.

- Spread half in bottom of greased 9 x 13-inch baking dish.

- Pour squash mixture over stuffing and cover with remaining stuffing mixture.

- Bake at 350° for 25 to 30 minutes.

Yield: 8 to 10 servings

Summer Garden Vegetables

½	cup butter or margarine	½	cup all-purpose flour
1	cup sliced onion	2	green peppers, chopped
1	clove garlic, minced	2	tomatoes, cut into wedges
2	yellow squash, cut into ½-inch pieces	½	teaspoon salt
		¼	tablespoon oregano
1	medium eggplant, peeled and cut into ½-inch pieces	⅛	tablespoon celery salt
		⅛	tablespoon pepper

- Melt butter in large skillet.
- Sauté onion and garlic until tender.
- Dredge squash and eggplant in flour to coat lightly.
- Add squash, eggplant and green peppers to onions.
- Cover and simmer for 30 minutes.
- Add tomatoes, salt, oregano, celery salt and pepper.
- Simmer an additional 20 minutes.

Yield: 6 to 8 servings

Hash Brown Surprise

1	(32-ounce) bag frozen hash brown potatoes	8	ounces sharp Cheddar cheese, grated
2	(10¾-ounce) cans potato soup	½	teaspoon garlic salt
1	(8-ounce) carton sour cream	½	cup Parmesan cheese
			Butter

- Mix together all ingredients except Parmesan cheese and butter.
- Place in a 2½-quart 13 x 9-inch buttered baking dish.
- Dot with butter and sprinkle with Parmesan cheese.
- Cook uncovered in a 350° oven for 1 hour.

Yield: 10 to 12 servings

"Ginny Gordon's Gifts and Gadgets" Potato Kugel

2	pounds all-purpose potatoes, peeled	1	teaspoon salt
2	medium carrots, peeled	1	teaspoon Cavender's Greek seasoning
1	medium onion, chopped	⅛	teaspoon black pepper
2	eggs, beaten	⅓	cup chicken fat or melted butter
2	tablespoons self-rising flour		

- Shred or grate potatoes and carrots with food processor or by hand.
- Add remaining ingredients, mix and pour into a greased 9 x 13-inch baking dish.
- Bake uncovered at 375° for 30 minutes.
- Serve immediately.

Yield: 6 to 8 servings

Famous Baked Potatoes

Baking potatoes   Rock salt, ground
Margarine, melted

- Brush whole, washed, raw baking potatoes with melted butter or margarine.
- Dust tops with rock salt.
- Place on baking sheet with salt facing up.
- Bake at 350° for 1 hour or until done.
- Serve with your favorite toppings.

Yield: 1 potato per person

Red Potato Casserole

3	pounds red potatoes, peeled and diced	1	(10¾-ounce) can cream of celery soup
¾	cup margarine, melted and divided	1	(8-ounce) carton sour cream
½	cup finely chopped onion	½	pound sharp Cheddar cheese, shredded
		2	cups corn flakes, crushed

- Boil potatoes until fork tender and drain.
- Mix with ½ cup melted margarine, onion, soup, sour cream and cheese.
- Pour into greased 2½-quart casserole.
- Mix crushed corn flakes and ¼ cup melted margarine. Sprinkle over potato mixture.
- Bake uncovered at 350° for about 50 minutes.

Yield: 10 to 12 servings

Mushroom or chicken soup may be substituted depending on what you are serving. Two cups of finely chopped ham may be added to make a main dish.

Boil and Bake Potatoes

An easier and quicker version of double-baked potatoes.

6	medium baking potatoes	1	pint sour cream
2	cups grated sharp Cheddar cheese	1	teaspoon salt
½	cup butter, melted	¼	teaspoon pepper

- Boil potatoes whole in jackets 30 to 40 minutes until fork tender; peel and grate.
- Combine 1½ cups cheese and all other ingredients.
- Put in 9 x 13-inch casserole and top with ½ cup cheese.
- Bake 40 minutes at 350°.

Yield: 8 to 10 servings

Optional additions could be chopped onions, bacon, chives, or parsley.

Sweet Potato Soufflé

3	cups cooked, mashed sweet potatoes	¼	teaspoon nutmeg
1	cup sugar	⅛	teaspoon cinnamon
¼	cup butter, melted	½	cup milk
2	eggs	1	cup brown sugar
¼	teaspoon salt	⅓	cup butter, melted
¼	teaspoon vanilla	⅓	cup flour
		1	cup chopped pecans

- Mix first 9 ingredients until well blended.
- Pour into 8 x 11-inch buttered baking dish.
- Mix brown sugar, butter, flour and nuts. Sprinkle on potato mixture.
- Bake at 350° for 30 to 35 minutes.

Yield: 6 to 8 servings

Grandma's Sweet Potato Pudding

4	cups grated raw sweet potatoes	1	teaspoon cinnamon
1½	cups sugar	1	teaspoon nutmeg
¾	stick butter, melted	1	lemon, grated rind and juice
2	eggs		Dash salt

- Scald potatoes with 4 cups boiling water for 5 minutes, drain.
- Mix all ingredients.
- Pour into 8 x 8-inch baking dish. Bake at 350° for 1½ hours.

Yield: 6 to 8 servings

Twice Baked Yams

6	medium yams (sweet potatoes)	¼	cup butter or margarine, melted
1	teaspoon salt		Orange juice
½	cup apricot preserves		Ground nutmeg

- Bake yams in 350° oven until done (about 1 hour).
- Cut yams in half and scoop out inside, careful not to break skin.
- In a mixing bowl, mash yams.
- Add preserves, butter and enough orange juice to moisten. Beat until fluffy.
- Pile into skins and sprinkle with nutmeg.
- Bake at 350° for 15 to 20 minutes.

Yield: 8 to 12 servings

Spinach Squares

1	cup flour	½	cup chopped onion
1	teaspoon salt		Dash garlic powder
1	teaspoon baking powder	2	eggs, beaten
1	(10-ounce) package chopped	1	cup milk
	spinach, thawed and drained	¼	cup butter, melted
8	ounces Cheddar cheese, grated		

- Mix flour, salt and baking powder together.
- Add spinach, cheese, onion and garlic powder to dry ingredients.
- Add eggs, milk and butter and mix well.
- Pour into greased 13 x 9-inch pan.
- Bake at 350° for 30 minutes.

Yield: 8 to 10 servings

Scalloped Spinach

2	(10-ounce) packages frozen chopped spinach	½	cup milk
2	tablespoons finely chopped onion	½	cup grated Parmesan cheese
		¼	teaspoon salt
			Dash pepper
2	eggs, beaten (may substitute egg beaters)	½	cup soft buttered bread crumbs

- Cook and drain spinach. Squeeze until very dry.
- Combine spinach with all other ingredients except bread crumbs.
- Pour into 2-quart baking dish. Top with crumbs.
- Bake at 350° for 30 minutes or until knife comes out clean.

Yield: 6 servings

Tomato Casserole

2	tablespoons butter	⅛	cup water
½	medium onion, chopped	2-3	slices bread, torn into small pieces
1	(28-ounce) can stewed tomatoes		
¼-⅜	cup sugar		Garlic powder
	Dash each celery salt, savory, basil, oregano		Cooking spray
		¼	cup grated cheese

- Sauté onion in butter.
- Combine with all other ingredients except bread crumbs and cheese.
- Pour into 2-quart or 8 x 11-inch buttered casserole.
- Top with garlic bread crumbs (sprinkle plain bread crumbs with garlic powder and spray with Pam) and grated cheese.
- Bake at 350° until bubbly.

Yield: 6 servings

Fried Green Tomatoes

1	egg, beaten	½	teaspoon pepper
½	cup milk	3	medium green tomatoes, cut in
½	cup cornmeal		⅓-inch slices
¼	cup all-purpose flour	3-4	tablespoons vegetable oil
1	teaspoon salt		

- Combine egg and milk; set aside.
- Combine cornmeal, flour, salt and pepper.
- Dip tomatoes in egg mixture; dredge in cornmeal mixture.
- Heat 3 tablespoons oil in large skillet over medium heat.
- Arrange a single layer of tomato slices in skillet and cook until golden brown on each side; set aside.
- Repeat with remaining slices, adding more oil if needed.

Yield: 6 servings

Braised Vegetables

3	carrots	1-2	tablespoons butter
1	onion	½	cup dry white vermouth
6	celery stalks		Salt and pepper to taste
1	turnip (optional)		

- Cut vegetables into julienne strips.
- Melt butter in heavy saucepan with a lid.
- Add vegetables and vermouth, salt and pepper and stir to mix.
- Place waxed paper over top touching vegetables.
- Cover and cook over moderately low heat 45 minutes or until vegetables are tender.

Yield: 4 servings

Chopped fresh ginger may be added for extra flavor.

Scalloped Tomatoes

2	tablespoons butter	½	teaspoon salt
½	cup chopped onion	¼	teaspoon pepper
½	cup chopped green pepper	2	tablespoons cornstarch
½	cup chopped celery	2	tablespoons vinegar
1	(28-ounce) can diced tomatoes	2	cups bread crumbs
¼-½	cup sugar	1	stick butter, melted
½	teaspoon basil		

- Melt butter in large skillet. Sauté onion, pepper and celery in butter.
- Add tomatoes, sugar and seasonings. Bring to boil.
- Mix cornstarch and vinegar in separate bowl and stir until smooth.
- Add this to tomato mixture. Mix well.
- Pour into buttered 2-quart casserole dish. Top with bread crumbs and butter mixture.
- Bake uncovered 30 minutes at 375°.

Yield: 6 to 8 servings

Zucchini Pie

1	large onion, chopped	3-4	tablespoons fresh parsley
1	cup grated cheese	1	teaspoon salt
½	cup oil	½	teaspoon pepper
1	cup biscuit mix	2	small zucchini, grated
4	eggs, beaten		

- Mix together all ingredients.
- Pour into 9-inch pie plate.
- Bake at 350° for 35 to 40 minutes.

Yield: 6 servings

Beth's Zesty Zucchini Bake

6	slices bacon	1	(8-ounce) carton sour cream
2	pounds medium zucchini, sliced thin	2	tablespoons flour
		1½	cups shredded sharp Cheddar cheese
1	(4-ounce) can sliced mushrooms		
1	onion, sliced		Garlic salt and pepper to taste
1	tablespoon butter, melted	½	cup fine Italian bread crumbs
2	eggs, separated	1	tablespoon butter, melted

- Cook bacon. Crumble and set aside.
- Put zucchini, mushrooms, onions and butter in skillet or heavy saucepan and cook over medium heat until tender, stirring occasionally.
- Beat egg yolks and sour cream.
- Add flour, stirring until blended.
- Beat egg whites until stiff; fold into sour cream mixture.
- In a 8 x 12-inch baking dish, layer ½ squash, then ½ of sour cream mixture, cheese, salt, pepper and bacon.
- Repeat layers and top with buttered bread crumbs.
- Bake at 350° for 25 minutes. Garnish with parsley or bacon bits.

Yield: 6 servings

Indian Summer Roasted Veggies with Two Cheeses

½	cup olive oil	1	large sweet onion, sliced in ¼-inch rounds
3-4	tablespoons balsamic vinegar	1	large red bell pepper, diced
½	teaspoon salt	1	medium zucchini, sliced in ¼-inch rounds
¼	teaspoon pepper		
1	tablespoon dry parsley	1	medium yellow squash, sliced in ¼-inch rounds
1	teaspoon dry minced garlic		
¼	teaspoon dry thyme	3	ripe tomatoes, sliced
1	tablespoon dry basil	¾	cup Parmesan cheese, grated
2	large baking potatoes, sliced in ¼-inch rounds	6	ounces extra sharp Cheddar cheese, grated

- Mix or whisk the first 8 ingredients very well.
- In a greased 9 x 13-inch dish, layer vegetables ending with tomatoes.
- On each layer, sprinkle first with herb/oil mixture, then Parmesan cheese.
- Sprinkle top with grated Cheddar cheese.
- Bake uncovered for 50 minutes at 350°.
- Cover lightly with foil and bake 10 more minutes.

Yield: 12 servings

Roasted Veggies with Herbs and Garlic

3 sweet potatoes, peeled and cut into 1-inch pieces
3 carrots, peeled and cut in large pieces
2 onions, peeled and cut into 8 wedges

1 garlic head, separated into cloves and peeled
¼ cup minced fresh rosemary
¼ cup minced fresh thyme leaves
3 tablespoons olive oil
Salt and pepper to taste

• Preheat oven to 400°.
• In a large bowl, toss vegetables and herbs.
• Add oil and toss again.
• Spread mixture on large baking sheet and bake, stirring occasionally for 1 hour.
• Add salt and pepper to taste.

Yield: 6 servings

Cheesy Pineapple Casserole

2 (15½-ounce) cans pineapple tidbits, drained
6 tablespoons flour
1 cup grated sharp Cheddar cheese

¾ cup sugar
1 stack Ritz crackers, crumbled
1 stick butter or margarine, melted

• Mix pineapple, flour, cheese and sugar until flour is moistened.
• Spread in greased 9 x 13-inch baking dish.
• Sprinkle with crackers and drizzle with butter.
• Bake at 350° for 25 to 30 minutes.

Yield: 8 to 10 servings

Can easily be halved.

Hot Fruit Compote

1	cup canned peach slices	2	tablespoons butter
1	cup canned pear slices	1	stick cinnamon
1	cup pineapple chunks	⅛	teaspoon nutmeg
½	cup orange marmalade	⅛	teaspoon ground cloves

- Drain fruit, reserving 1½ cups syrup.
- Combine marmalade, butter, spices and reserved syrup in heavy saucepan.
- Bring to boil and cook 2 to 3 minutes.
- Reduce heat and add fruit. Simmer for 20 minutes.

Yield: 6 servings

Great for brunch or breakfast or as a side dish with pork.

Baked Fruit Casserole

1	(16-ounce) can sliced peaches	2	tablespoons cornstarch
1	(16-ounce) can pineapple chunks	½	cup brown sugar
1	(16-ounce) can pear halves or slices	¼	cup butter
		½	cup sherry
1	(14-ounce) jar spiced apple rings	2	teaspoons curry (optional)

- Drain fruit thoroughly saving to make 2 cups.
- Add cornstarch, brown sugar, butter and sherry to juices.
- Cook in saucepan until thickened. Add curry if desired.
- Arrange fruit in casserole with apple rings on top. Pour thickened sauce over all.
- Bake at 350° for 20 minutes.

Yield: 8 servings

Can use any combination of fruits desired. Great for brunch.

Stuffing for Anything

A great accompaniment for meats or just as a side dish.

4	tablespoons butter	7	cups cornbread stuffing mix
1½	cups finely chopped onions	1	teaspoon garlic
1½	cups finely chopped green peppers	4	cups crumbled toast
3-4	jalapeño peppers	3	hard-boiled eggs, finely chopped
1	cup chopped celery	2	cups creamed corn
1	cup sliced mushrooms	2	cups grated extra-sharp Cheddar cheese
1	cup chopped leeks		Chicken or turkey broth
1	pound hot sausage, cooked		

- Cook vegetables in butter until tender. Transfer to large mixing bowl.
- Add remaining ingredients, except broth, and mix well.
- Stir in broth (about 1 cup) until mixture is consistency of cake batter.
- Pour into 9 x 13-inch pan and bake at 350° for 25 minutes; do not overcook.
- If too dry, add more broth.

Yield: 8 to 10 servings

Main Dishes

Cross the Cut - Watercolor

Lynda Fodrie Steed, 1940-2000

Mrs. Steed was a Beaufort native and member of St. Paul's. She began studying art as a child but postponed serious study until the 1960's. She lived in Virginia at that time and began winning art shows in several states. She was also in great demand for the sale of her work. Mrs. Steed owned and operated an artist's co-op where she also taught. When she returned to Beaufort in 1979 to operate the Net House Restaurant, she put art on hold except for some personal work. She served on the Art Committee for this cookbook.

Chicken and Broccoli Casserole

A wonderful Fall Bazaar luncheon dish that can be easily increased to feed a crowd.

1	(4-pound) chicken	2	(4-ounce) cans mushrooms,
2	(10-ounce) packages frozen		stems and juice
	broccoli spears	1	(2-ounce) jar pimentos, drained
1	(10¾-ounce) can cream of	1	(8-ounce) carton sour cream
	chicken soup	1	cup real mayonnaise
1	(10¾-ounce) can cream of	1	tablespoon lemon juice
	mushroom soup	¾	cup grated sharp Cheddar cheese
		1	cup buttered bread crumbs

- Cook chicken and cut into pieces.
- Cook broccoli and drain well.
- Mix soup, mushrooms, pimentos, sour cream, mayonnaise and lemon juice.
- Layer broccoli, chicken, soup mixture, cheese and bread crumbs.
- Bake at 350° until bubbly, about 30 to 40 minutes.
- Serve with rice.

Yield: 10 servings

Swiss Chicken Casserole

6	boneless chicken breast halves	¼	cup milk
6	slices Swiss cheese	2	cups seasoned stuffing mix
1	(10¾-ounce) can cream of	¼	cup butter or margarine, melted
	chicken soup		

- Arrange chicken breasts in a lightly greased 8 x 11-inch baking dish.
- Top with cheese slices.
- Combine soup with milk, stir well. Spoon sauce over chicken.
- Sprinkle with stuffing mix. Drizzle butter over crumbs.
- Cover and bake at 350° for 50 minutes.

Yield: 6 servings

Can be made ahead and frozen.

Chicken Broccoli Crescent Braid

3	boneless chicken breasts, cooked	½	cup shredded sharp Cheddar cheese
1	cup chopped fresh broccoli	½	cup mayonnaise
½	cup chopped red pepper (can be ¼ red and ¼ green)	½	cup sour cream
		2	packages refrigerated crescent rolls
¼	cup chopped onion		
½	cup sliced fresh mushrooms	1	egg white, beaten

- Chop chicken and broccoli and add next 4 ingredients to a 4-quart mixing bowl.

- Mix gently and add the mayonnaise and sour cream. Set aside.

- Open the crescent rolls. Unroll but do not separate. Press dough in a 12 x 15-inch pan or baking stone. Seal all perforations.

- On longest sides, cut dough into strips 1½-inch apart and 3-inches deep. There will be 6 inches in center to put the chicken broccoli mixture.

- To braid, lift strips across mixture to meet in center, twisting each 1 turn. Tuck ends under to seal at each end.

- Brush egg white over dough after braid is ready for oven.

- Bake 25 to 28 minutes at 375°. Cut and serve.

Yield: 6 servings

Chicken Curry

¼	cup chopped onion	2	teaspoons curry powder
3	cups unpeeled chopped tart apples	1	cup skim milk
1	tablespoon oil	1½	cups cooked chicken, diced
2	tablespoons flour	¼	cup raisins
½	teaspoon salt		Red pepper flakes to taste
⅛	teaspoon ground ginger	2	cups rice, cooked and unsalted

- Cook onions and apples in oil until tender.
- Stir in flour, salt, ginger and curry powder.
- Add milk slowly, stirring constantly, cook until thickened.
- Add chicken, raisins and red pepper flakes; heat to serving temperature.
- Serve over cooked rice.

Yield: 4 servings

Pass small chopped condiments - raisins, chutney, salted peanuts, toasted coconut, dried apricots, chopped onion.

Oven Barbecued Chicken

8	chicken breast halves	2	tablespoons sugar
2	tablespoons vegetable oil	½	cup ketchup
3	tablespoons Worcestershire sauce		Few drops Tabasco sauce
2	tablespoons vinegar	1	medium onion, chopped
		1	garlic clove

- Wash chicken; remove skin, dry and brown in vegetable oil.
- Remove from skillet and place in a 9 x 13-inch baking dish.
- Mix remaining ingredients and pour over chicken.
- Bake covered at 350° for 1 hour.

Yield: 6 to 8 servings

Company Chicken

8	boneless skinless chicken breast halves	1	(8-ounce) bottle Russian dressing
1	envelope dry onion soup mix	1	(10-ounce) jar apricot preserves

- Preheat oven to 325°.
- Spray 9 x 13-inch baking dish with nonstick spray. Place chicken in baking dish.
- Mix together onion soup mix, Russian dressing and preserves. Pour over chicken.
- Cover with foil and bake at 325° for 45 minutes.
- Remove foil and bake 15 minutes.
- May be served over rice.

Yield: 6 to 8 servings

Annie B's Barbecued Chicken

1	cup white vinegar	2	teaspoons black pepper
½	cup water	1-2	tablespoons salt, or to taste
¼	pound butter		Zest and juice of 1 lemon
2-3	tablespoons crushed red pepper, or to taste	3-4	pounds chicken pieces
¼	teaspoon Worcestershire sauce		Salt and pepper

- Combine first 8 ingredients in saucepan and bring to a boil. Simmer for at least 1 hour to blend flavors.
- Salt and pepper chicken pieces. Place in 9 x 13-inch pan, skin side up.
- Bake at 325° to 350° for 1 hour.
- Turn chicken over and add sauce.
- Continue baking additional hour, basting several times.
- Turn chicken once more, reduce heat to 200°, continue basting and allow chicken pieces to brown.

Yield: 8 to 10 servings

Chicken Alfredo

3 eggs	3 tablespoons butter
2 tablespoons water	2 tablespoons olive oil
6 boneless skinless chicken breast halves	2 cups heavy cream
½ cup flour	½ cup water
Salt and pepper to taste	½ cup butter
½ cup Romano cheese	1 cup Romano cheese
¼ cup chopped parsley	1 (8-ounce) package egg noodles
1 cup bread crumbs	Parsley
½ teaspoon salt	Parmesan cheese

- Mix 3 eggs and 2 tablespoons water for egg wash and set aside.
- Dust chicken with flour, salt and pepper.
- In separate bowl, mix cheese, parsley, bread crumbs and salt.
- Dip chicken in egg wash and then in cheese mixture.
- Sauté chicken in butter and oil for 15 minutes over medium heat.
- Place in 9 x 13-inch baking dish.
- Combine cream, water, butter and cheese in a saucepan and heat, do not boil.
- Pour this over chicken and bake at 325° for 30 minutes.
- Cook noodles as directed on package.
- To serve, place chicken over noodles and pour sauce over, sprinkle with parsley.
- Can sprinkle with ½ cup Parmesan cheese before baking.

Yield: 4 to 6 servings

Chicken and Beef Casserole
An old and quick standby that is delicious!

1 (2.25-ounce) jar dried beef
8-10 boneless skinless chicken
    breast halves
8-10 bacon slices

1 (10¾-ounce) can cream of
    mushroom soup
1 (8-ounce) carton sour cream

- Line 9 x 13-inch baking dish with dried beef.
- Wrap chicken pieces with bacon and place in dish.
- Mix soup and sour cream and spread over chicken.
- Bake uncovered at 300° for 3 hours.

Yield: 6 to 8 servings

Cosmopolitan Chicken

½ pint sour cream
2 tablespoons lemon juice
2 tablespoons Worcestershire
    sauce
1 teaspoon celery salt

½ teaspoon garlic salt
    Paprika and pepper to taste
    Herb-seasoned stuffing mix
6 boneless chicken breast halves
1 stick butter, melted

- Mix sour cream, lemon juice, Worcestershire sauce, salts, paprika and pepper together.
- Crush stuffing mix into fine crumbs and set aside.
- Dip chicken into sour cream mixture and then into crumbs to completely coat.
- Place chicken in 9 x 13-inch baking dish and drizzle with butter.
- Bake uncovered at 350° for 1 hour or until brown and tender.

Yield: 6 servings

Can be prepared a day ahead, refrigerated and butter added before baking.

Chicken with Creamy Herb Sauce

6	boneless skinless chicken breast halves	3	tablespoons reduced-calorie mayonnaise
⅓	cup balsamic vinegar	1	tablespoon water
1	teaspoon dried oregano	1½	teaspoons fresh minced thyme or ½ teaspoon dried
½	teaspoon salt		
½	teaspoon pepper	⅛	teaspoon salt
3	cloves garlic, unpeeled	⅛	teaspoon pepper
¼	cup low fat buttermilk		Thyme sprigs (optional)
2	tablespoons fresh minced parsley		

- Arrange chicken in single layer in 9 x 13-inch baking dish.

- Pour vinegar over chicken and sprinkle with oregano, salt and pepper; add garlic cloves.

- Bake at 325° degrees for 25 minutes, basting occasionally with pan drippings. Remove from oven but keep chicken warm.

- Remove garlic and peel. Place garlic in bowl and mash into a paste.

- Add buttermilk and remaining ingredients and stir with a wire whisk until blended.

- Cut each breast diagonally across grain into thin slices.

- Arrange 1 breast on each of 6 plates. Spoon 1½ tablespoons sauce on top.

- Garnish with thyme and serve immediately.

Yield: 6 servings

Hot Chicken Salad

A tasty way to use leftover chicken or turkey!

2½ cups diced cooked chicken or turkey
1½ cups diced celery
½ cup blanched almonds, slivered and diced
½ teaspoon salt
Pepper to taste
2 tablespoons grated onion
1 tablespoon lemon juice

¾ cup mayonnaise
½ cup sour cream
2 hard-boiled eggs, chopped
1 cup shredded sharp Cheddar cheese
1 cup broken potato chips
½ cup water chestnuts (optional)
¼ cup diced pimento (optional)

- Mix together all ingredients except cheese and chips.
- Turn into a buttered 8 x 11-inch baking dish.
- Sprinkle cheese, then potato chips on top.
- Bake uncovered at 375° for 20 minutes until bubbly.

Yield: 6 to 8 servings

Szechuan Spicy Cold Noodles

A great potluck dish that is different!

1 (1-pound) package linguine
6 tablespoons creamy peanut butter
6 tablespoons light soy sauce
4 tablespoons sesame oil
4 tablespoons red wine vinegar
4 teaspoons sugar

2 teaspoons "hot oil" (China Bowl brand of red oil, hot sauce, or chili)
8 ounces chicken, cooked and sliced into thin strips
6 scallions, cut into short lengths

- Cook linguine as directed, drain and rinse with cold water.
- Combine peanut butter, soy sauce, sesame oil, vinegar, sugar and hot oil; mix until smooth.
- Toss with linguine.
- Top with slices of chicken and sprinkle with scallions.

Yield: 6 to 8 servings

Chicken Divan

1	(3½ to 4-pound) chicken or pieces	1½	teaspoons lemon juice
2	(10-ounce) packages frozen broccoli, thawed	¾	teaspoon curry powder
2	(10¾-ounce) cans cream of chicken soup	½	cup shredded sharp Cheddar cheese
1	cup mayonnaise	¾	cup herb-seasoned stuffing mix
			Butter

- Cook chicken in water until tender. Skin, bone and chop into bite-size pieces.
- Place broccoli in lightly greased 11 x 7-inch baking dish.
- Top with chicken.
- Combine soup, mayonnaise, lemon juice and curry powder. Pour over chicken.
- Sprinkle with cheese and stuffing mix. Dot with butter.
- Bake at 400° for 30 minutes or until thoroughly heated.

Yield: 4 to 6 servings

Chicken and Cheese Bake

4	whole boneless chicken breasts, halved	½	cup dry white wine
4	slices Swiss cheese	1	cup herb seasoned stuffing mix, crushed
4	slices provolone cheese	½	stick margarine, melted
1	(10¾-ounce) can cream of chicken soup		

- Grease 9 x 13-inch baking dish and place chicken in single layer.
- Top with cheeses.
- Combine soup and wine and pour over cheese.
- Sprinkle crumbs over all and drizzle with margarine.
- Bake uncovered at 350° for 50 minutes.

Yield: 6 to 8 servings

Chicken Mediterranean

6-10 boneless skinless chicken
    breast halves
1   cup flour seasoned with salt
    and pepper
1   cup chopped onion
1   cup chopped celery
½   cup sliced green pepper,
    1½-inch pieces
½   cup sliced yellow pepper,
    1½-inch pieces

2   tablespoons olive oil
5-6 Roma tomatoes, scalded,
    skinned and chopped
1-2 (4-ounce) cans sliced
    mushrooms
½   teaspoon minced garlic
½-1 teaspoon Italian seasoning
1   teaspoon Worcestershire sauce
20   black olives, sliced

- Shake chicken breasts in lightly seasoned flour.
- Brown on both sides in olive oil.
- Place in greased or sprayed 9 x 13-inch casserole.
- Sauté vegetables in olive oil until crisp/tender.
- Add tomatoes with juice, mushrooms, seasonings and Worcestershire sauce.
- Simmer 5 minutes to blend flavors.
- Mix in olives.
- Pour over chicken and cover tightly with foil.
- Bake at 325° for 45 minutes to 1 hour or until chicken is very tender but holds its shape.
- Serve with or over rice or pasta.

Yield: 6 to 8 servings

Chicken Piccata

1	tablespoon butter		Salt and pepper
1	tablespoon flour	2	tablespoons olive oil
4	whole boneless skinless	2-4	tablespoons butter
	chicken breasts	½	cup dry white wine or vermouth
	Juice of 1 lemon	1	cup chicken broth
	Flour		Chopped fresh parsley

- Melt 1 tablespoon butter in small saucepan.

- Add 1 tablespoon flour and cook over medium heat for several minutes. Set aside.

- Cut each breast in half and pound until thin. Sprinkle with lemon juice; dust with flour and season with salt and pepper.

- Heat oil and butter in heavy skillet until hot.

- Add chicken pieces to fit in one layer without crowding. Sauté 2 to 3 minutes on each side or until golden brown.

- Remove and keep warm while cooking remaining chicken. Add more butter or oil as needed. Remove to platter.

- Deglaze pan with wine and broth, bring to a boil and add butter and flour mixture to thicken.

- Boil for several minutes until thickened and smooth.

- Taste for seasoning and add few drops of lemon juice if needed.

- Pour sauce over chicken and sprinkle with parsley.

Yield: 4 to 6 servings

Cornish Hens and Rice

2	cups rice	1	package dry Italian salad
4	cups boiling water		dressing
2	(10¾-ounce) cans cream of	4	Cornish hens split
	chicken soup		

- Spread rice in 2 shallow 11 x 8-inch greased baking dishes.
- Bake at 350 degrees for 20 minutes or until rice is golden brown.
- Combine liquids and dry dressing in large mixing bowl and stir in browned rice.
- Divide in half and return to baking dishes.
- Place hens; cut side down, on rice.
- Bake at 350° for 1 hour; if hens become too brown, cover with foil.

Yield: 6 servings

Mexican Turkey

1	pound ground turkey	1	(16-ounce) can Mexican style
2	tablespoons oil		tomatoes
1	package taco seasoning	1	(6½-ounce) package cornbread
½	cup water		mix
1	(16-ounce) can kidney beans,	½	cup chopped onions
	drained	½	cup grated cheese
		½	cup chopped jalapeño peppers

- In a large skillet, brown turkey in oil.
- Stir in taco seasoning and water. Simmer 10 minutes.
- Spread beans in 8 x 8-inch baking dish. Spread turkey mixture over beans and add tomatoes.
- Prepare cornbread mix per directions; stir in onions, cheese and jalapeño peppers.
- Spread over tomatoes to completely cover.
- Bake uncovered at 350° until golden brown, about 30 to 40 minutes.

Yield: 6 servings

Turkey and Broccoli with Rice

1	cup cooked rice	1½	cups coarsely chopped cooked turkey
1	medium onion, chopped		
1	medium-size green pepper, chopped	1	(10¾-ounce) can cream of mushroom soup
2	stalks celery, chopped	1	(8-ounce) can sliced water chestnuts, drained
3	tablespoons butter or margarine, melted	1	cup shredded Cheddar cheese
1	(10-ounce) package frozen broccoli spears	½	cup shredded jalapeño cheese
		½	teaspoon salt
		¼	teaspoon pepper

- Cook rice according to directions.

- Sauté onion, green pepper and celery in butter in a large skillet until vegetables are tender, set aside.

- Cook broccoli according to package directions and drain.

- Cut spears in half and arrange in a greased shallow 2-quart casserole.

- Combine sautéed vegetables and remaining ingredients; spoon over broccoli.

- Bake uncovered at 350° for 30 minutes or until heated.

Yield: 4 to 6 servings

Bourbon Braised Pork Chops

½ cup all-purpose flour
½ teaspoon salt
¼ teaspoon pepper
4 (1-inch) thick pork chops
1 tablespoon vegetable oil
2 tablespoons brown sugar
2 tablespoons cornstarch
⅛ teaspoon ground allspice

1 cup hot water
¼ cup orange juice
2 tablespoons bourbon
¼ cup raisins (optional)
4 orange slices
2 extra tablespoons bourbon
   (optional)

- Combine first 3 ingredients and dredge pork chops in mixture to lightly coat.
- Brown pork chops on both sides in vegetable oil in large skillet.
- Combine brown sugar, cornstarch and allspice; slowly stir in hot water.
- Add orange juice, bourbon, raisins and orange slices.
- Add mixture to pork chops in skillet.
- Cover and simmer 50 to 55 minutes or until tender.

Yield: 4 servings

If desired, flambé pork chops with 2 tablespoons bourbon in serving dish.

Different Baked Ham

2 cups diced ham	½ teaspoon sage
4 tablespoons butter	Salt and pepper to taste
2 cups chopped onions	1 cup sour cream
½ pound fresh mushrooms, sliced	1½ cups fresh bread crumbs
½ teaspoon thyme	

- Sauté ham in 2 tablespoons butter.
- Add onions and remaining butter and cook until onions are tender.
- Add mushrooms and mix well. Add seasonings.
- Mix sour cream with 1 cup bread crumbs and add to ham mixture.
- Place in greased 1-quart baking dish. Top with remaining bread crumbs.
- Bake at 350° for 20 minutes.

Yield: 4 servings

Grilled Pork Tenderloin

2 (¾-pound) pork tenderloins	2 tablespoons brown sugar
⅓ cup soy sauce	3 tablespoons honey
½ teaspoon ground ginger	2 teaspoons dark sesame oil
5 cloves garlic, halved	

- Place tenderloins in shallow container or large plastic zip top bag.
- Combine soy sauce, ginger and garlic. Pour over tenderloins.
- Refrigerate for at least 3 hours, turning occasionally.
- Remove tenderloins from marinade and discard marinade.
- Combine brown sugar, honey and oil in a small saucepan. Cook over low heat, stirring until sugar is dissolved.
- Place tenderloins on grill rack and brush with honey mixture.
- Cook 20 minutes, turning once and basting frequently with honey mixture. Keep honey mixture warm.

Yield: 4 to 6 servings

Greek Pork Pita Pockets

4	tablespoons olive oil	2	pita leaves or rounds
4	tablespoons lemon juice	1	cup plain yogurt
1	tablespoon prepared mustard	1	cucumber, peeled and chopped finely
2	cloves garlic, minced		
1-2	teaspoons oregano	½	teaspoon crushed garlic
1	pound pork loin, cut into thin strips	½	teaspoon dill
			Red onions, chopped finely

- Make a marinade of first 5 ingredients.

- Pour over pork strips and marinate in refrigerator for 1 to 8 hours.

- Remove and stir-fry in nonstick pan over medium heat for 2 to 5 minutes or until no longer pink.

- Halve 2 pita leaves and open to form a pocket. Fill with pork.

- Combine and mix well yogurt, cucumber, garlic and dill.

- Top pork filled pita with cucumber sauce.

- Garnish with red onions.

Yield: 4 servings

Chinese Pork Tenderloin

1	package whole pork tenderloin (2 pieces)	¾	cup sugar
½	cup soy sauce	1	(1-inch) piece gingerroot, peeled and minced
½	cup ketchup	1	clove garlic, minced
½	cup sherry		

- Place pork in dish large enough for marinating.
- Mix remaining ingredients and pour over pork.
- Marinate in refrigerator for 2 hours. Turn loins at least twice while marinating.
- Remove pork from marinade and cook on grill or covered in oven at 325° for 45 minutes.
- While pork is cooking, place marinade in saucepan and cook until it is reduced to half.
- Slice pork and serve sauce over top or on side.

Yield: 4 to 6 servings

This sauce and marinade is also great for spareribs.

Braised Medallions of Pork Tenderloin

1	tablespoon butter			Salt and pepper
1	tablespoon flour			Flour
½	pound fresh mushrooms, sliced		½	cup vermouth
2	scallions or shallots, minced		1	cup chicken broth
1	clove garlic, minced		¼	teaspoon thyme
2	tablespoons olive oil			Chopped fresh parsley
1½	pounds pork tenderloin			Rice

- Melt butter over medium heat in small saucepan.

- Add flour and continue to heat several minutes. Set aside.

- In a large skillet, sauté mushrooms, scallions and garlic in 1 tablespoon olive oil. Remove from pan and set aside.

- Trim excess fat from pork and cut into ½-inch slices. Salt and pepper and dredge in flour.

- In same skillet, add remaining oil and sauté pork over medium high heat until lightly browned, 2 to 3 minutes on each side.

- Remove from pan and set aside.

- Deglaze pan with vermouth and chicken broth. Bring to boil and add Buerre Manie (cooked flour).

- Stir until smooth and add thyme.

- Return other ingredients to pan, cover and simmer for 20 minutes.

- Garnish with parsley and serve with rice.

Yield: 4 servings

Donnie's One Pot Dinner

1	medium cabbage, cut into eighths	1	pound Hillshire sausage or Kielbasa, cut into 4-inch links
4	medium potatoes, peeled and quartered	1½	cups water
			Salt and pepper to taste

- Place cabbage in bottom of 4-quart pot.
- Add salt and pepper and 1½ cups water.
- Place potatoes on cabbage. Place sausage on potatoes.
- Cover and bring to a full boil.
- Reduce heat to low and cook until potatoes are tender, about 20 to 25 minutes.
- Drain and place on platter with sausage in middle and cabbage and potatoes on each end.

Yield: 4 servings

Can be increased by using larger cabbage, a potato per person and ¼ pound sausage for each person and more water as volume in pot grows.

Roast Leg of Lamb

6-7	pounds leg of lamb	4	slices salt pork
1	garlic clove	2	cups hot coffee
	Salt and pepper to taste	½	pint half-and-half or evaporated
2	tablespoons dry mustard		milk

- Rub roast with garlic. Season well with salt, pepper and dry mustard.
- Place slices of salt pork over lamb, fasten with toothpicks.
- Roast at 450° for 30 minutes. Remove toothpicks and pork slices.
- Pour coffee and cream over lamb.
- Turn oven to 300°. Roast for 3 hours, basting every 15 to 30 minutes with drippings.
- Strain and remove grease from delicious gravy.

Yield: 8 to 10 servings

Chaucer's Lamb

½ cup Dijon mustard
2 tablespoons soy sauce
½ teaspoon tarragon
3 tablespoons olive oil
½ teaspoon dried thyme

½ teaspoon dried rosemary
1 large cloves garlic, minced
   Ground pepper and salt to taste
3-5 pound leg of lamb or
   tenderloins

- Mix mustard and soy sauce.
- Combine this mixture with remaining ingredients for marinade and mix well.
- Let mixture stand for an hour or so.
- Paint marinade liberally over lamb and allow to marinate for at least 1½ hours.
- Bake at 400° for 30 minutes and then reduce heat to 350° for an additional 30 minutes.

Yield: 4 to 6 servings

Fresh herbs can be used, but increase amount to 2 teaspoons of each herb. Marinade can also be used for pork, beef, or chicken.

Grilled Leg of Lamb

½ leg of lamb, butterflied
¼ cup olive oil
2 tablespoons fresh dill

1 clove garlic, minced
   Salt and pepper

- Two hours before grilling, place lamb on platter and brush with olive oil.
- Sprinkle lamb with dill, add garlic, salt and pepper and marinate for 2 hours.
- Cook on grill until done, 30 to 50 minutes, or until roasted on outside, pink inside.

Yield: 4 servings

Ann Byrd's Grilled
Butterflied Leg of Lamb

4	cloves garlic, minced	¼	cup olive oil
1	teaspoon black pepper	6	pound leg of butterflied lamb
¼	cup Worcestershire sauce	1	tablespoon rosemary
⅔	cup lemon juice	⅔	cup Dijon mustard
1	teaspoon salt		

- Combine first 6 ingredients and mix well.
- Place lamb in above mixture and marinate in refrigerator for 24 hours, turning frequently.
- Place lamb on grill over medium coals. Sprinkle rosemary on coals to add flavor.
- Cook lamb 20 to 30 minutes, brushing the surface with mustard and marinade.
- Turn meat; brush with remaining mustard and marinade.
- Cook 20 to 30 minutes for medium rare. Remove meat from grill and let rest 15 to 20 minutes.

Yield: 6 to 8 servings

For gas grill, cook 15 to 20 minutes each side for medium rare.

Lamb Shish Kebabs

4-5	pound leg of lamb	½	cup extra virgin olive oil
4	cloves of garlic, minced		Juice of ½ lemon
2	tablespoons minced onion	1	teaspoon curry
2-3	jalapeño peppers, minced or	1	teaspoon turmeric
	1 teaspoon dried red pepper	1	teaspoon salt

- Cut lamb into 1½-inch cubes.
- Mix marinade of remaining ingredients and pour over cubed lamb.
- Marinate for at least 4 hours.
- Thread lamb on skewers and grill until slightly pink inside, about 30 minutes, depending on grill.

Yield: 6 to 8 servings

Marinated Beef Tenderloin

	Freshly ground pepper	6	ounces soy sauce
3-5	pound beef tenderloin	1	ounce Worcestershire sauce
2	ounces Kitchen Bouquet		

- Rub beef tenderloin with desired amount of ground pepper.
- Mix Kitchen Bouquet, soy sauce and Worcestershire sauce together.
- Marinate beef 1 to 2 hours, not longer.
- Preheat oven to 450°. Cook uncovered 20 minutes.
- Turn oven off. Do not open door. Leave 15 minutes.
- Remove from oven and let rest up to 1 hour.

Yield: 6 to 10 servings

Rouladen

3	pounds top round steak, sliced ½-inch thick, pounded to ¼-inch thick	3	tablespoons canola oil
		2	cups water
		1	cup chopped celery
6	teaspoons Dijon mustard	¼	cup chopped onion
¼	cup finely chopped onion	3	parsley sprigs
6	slices bacon	1	tablespoon margarine
3	dill pickles, rinsed and cut lengthwise into halves	2	tablespoons flour

- Cut steak into 6 rectangular pieces about 4 x 8 inches.
- Spread each with teaspoon of mustard, sprinkle with 2 teaspoons onion.
- Place 1 bacon strip down center of each. Lay ½ pickle down narrow edge.
- Roll each piece of meat into cylinder. Secure with Rouladen clips or kitchen cord.
- In 12-inch skillet, brown rolls on all sides in oil. Transfer rolls to plate.
- Pour water into skillet and bring to boil. Add celery, ¼ cup onion and parsley.
- Return rolls to skillet, cover and simmer for 1 hour or until meat is tender.
- Remove rolls and cover with foil to keep warm.
- Strain cooking liquid and boil to reduce to 2 cups.
- Melt butter in saucepan. Sprinkle in flour and cook stirring constantly until golden brown.
- Gradually add cooking liquid and whisk until thick.
- Return rolls to skillet.
- Simmer over low heat only long enough to heat rolls thoroughly.

Yield: 6 servings

Beef Burgundy Provençale

A favorite ECW Bazaar frozen food seller!

6	strips bacon	1	cup burgundy
3	pounds lean boneless beef, cut into 1-inch cubes.	4	carrots, peeled and sliced
		1	teaspoon tomato paste
⅓	cup flour, seasoned with ½ teaspoon salt and ¼ teaspoon pepper	1	teaspoon herbs de Provence (or mixture of basil, thyme, parsley, etc.)
2	cups chopped onions	1	tablespoon green peppercorns (optional)
8	ounces fresh mushrooms		
1	clove garlic, minced	7-8	pearl onions (optional)
1¼	cups beef broth		

- In a large heavy pot with a lid or Dutch oven, fry bacon until crisp and remove.

- Dredge beef in flour and brown in bacon drippings and remove.

- Sauté onion, mushrooms and garlic in drippings.

- Add beef, broth, wine, carrots, herbs, peppercorns and tomato paste, adjusting seasonings.

- Cover and simmer over lowest heat for 2 to 2½ hours or until meat is very tender; stir occasionally. (Can be placed in covered casserole and baked at 300° for 2 hours.)

- Serve over rice, garnish with bacon and watercress; freezes well.

Yield: 8 to 10 servings

Steak in a Paper Bag

Sure to please the men in the house!

2 sirloin strip steaks, ½-inch thick
2 tablespoons vegetable oil
1 tablespoon salt
2 tablespoons freshly ground pepper

2 cloves garlic, finely chopped
1 cup coarse bread crumbs
1 brown paper bag

- Rub steaks well with oil, salt, pepper and garlic.
- Press the bread crumbs into the steaks to form a thick coating.
- Put carefully into paper bag and tie closed with string.
- Roast in a 375° oven for 35 to 40 minutes for rare, about 10 to 15 minutes longer for medium or well done.

Yield: 4 servings

Brisket of Beef

3-4 pounds of fresh beef brisket
Lawry's seasoned salt
Garlic salt
Paprika

Salt and pepper
1 onion, sliced
2 cups boiling water

- Place brisket in roasting pan. Rub with seasonings.
- Brown uncovered at 350° for 1 hour.
- Cover brisket with onion; add water and seal with foil or lid cover.
- Cook 4 to 5 hours at 300°. Check occasionally to make sure there is water in pan and add more water if needed.
- Cool and refrigerate overnight. Slice thinly across grain to serve.

Yield: 6 to 8 servings

Steak with Brandied Sauce

1½	pounds sirloin steaks, 1-inch thick, trimmed of fat	¼	cup brandy
2	teaspoons whole peppercorns	2	tablespoons chopped fresh parsley
2	tablespoons margarine, divided	2	tablespoons chopped fresh chives
1	tablespoon olive oil		

- Wipe steak dry with paper towel.
- Crush peppercorns and press into both sides of steak.
- Cover with waxed paper and refrigerate for 2 hours.
- Heat 1 tablespoon margarine with olive oil in a large skillet.
- Sauté steak until desired doneness and remove to a heated platter.
- Pour off fat from skillet then add 1 tablespoon margarine and brandy.
- Bring to a boil and cook 1 minute.
- Spoon sauce over steak and sprinkle with parsley and chives. Serve immediately.

Yield: 4 servings

1 small can of mushrooms can be added and sautéed before draining off fat.

Beef Tips

2	pounds lean stew beef	1	can water chestnuts, drained
1	(4-ounce) can mushrooms or fresh sliced	¾	cup sherry
		1	envelope dry onion soup mix
2	(10¾-ounce) cans cream of mushroom soup		

- Mix all ingredients, except onion soup mix.
- Pour into ungreased 3-quart casserole.
- Sprinkle onion soup mix on top.
- Cover and bake at 325° for 2 hours. Reduce heat to 300° and bake for 1 hour.
- Add splash more of sherry if sauce becomes too dry.
- Serve over or with rice or noodles.

Yield: 6 servings

Saucy Meat Loaf

1½	pounds ground beef	1	(15-ounce) can tomato sauce, divided
1	cup soft bread crumbs		
1	egg, beaten	2	tablespoons prepared mustard
1	medium onion, chopped	2	tablespoons brown sugar
½	green pepper, chopped	¼	cup water
1½	teaspoons salt	3	strips bacon (optional)
½	teaspoon pepper		

- Mix beef, crumbs, egg, onion, green pepper, salt, pepper and ½ can tomato sauce until well blended.
- Form into a loaf and place in shallow 8 x 11-inch baking dish.
- Bake at 350° for 15 minutes.
- Combine remaining tomato sauce, mustard, brown sugar and water.
- Pour over loaf. Add bacon on top and continue to bake 1 hour, basting frequently.

Yield: 4 to 6 servings

Hilton Head Casserole

8	ounces small pasta shells	1	(4-ounce) can sliced
2	pounds ground beef		mushrooms, undrained
2	medium onions, chopped	12	ounces sour cream
2	cloves garlic, minced	½	pound provolone cheese, sliced
1	pound chopped stewed	8	ounces mozzarella cheese,
	tomatoes		shredded
1	(14-ounce) can tomato sauce	½	cup Parmesan cheese
	Salt and pepper to taste		

- Cook pasta shells, rinse and drain.
- Brown beef, add onion and cook until soft.
- Add garlic, tomatoes, tomato sauce, mushrooms, salt and pepper. Simmer 20 minutes.
- In a 3-quart casserole, put enough sauce to cover bottom.
- Add layer of 2 cups pasta, then ½ of remaining sauce, ½ sour cream and ¼ pound of provolone.
- Repeat layers.
- Sprinkle with mozzarella; cover and bake at 350° for 40 minutes.
- Remove cover and continue baking until mozzarella melts.
- Remove from oven; sprinkle with Parmesan and let sit for 10 minutes.

Yield: 6 to 8 servings

Speedy Taco Bake

1	pound ground beef	2	cups shredded sharp Cheddar
½	cup chopped onion		cheese
2	tablespoons oil	2	cups biscuit mix
1	envelope taco seasoning mix	1	cup milk
1	(15-ounce) can tomato sauce	2	eggs
1	(15-ounce) can whole kernel		Sour cream
	corn, drained		Chopped tomatoes
			Shredded lettuce

- Cook beef and onion in oil in large skillet and drain.
- Add dry seasoning mix, tomato sauce and corn. Mix well.
- Spoon into 9 x 13-inch baking dish and sprinkle with cheese.
- Stir biscuit mix, milk and eggs together until blended and pour over beef mixture.
- Bake at 350° for 35 minutes or until golden brown.
- Serve with sour cream, chopped tomatoes and shredded lettuce.

Yield: 6 to 8 servings

Cheesy Beef Enchiladas

1 pound ground beef	1 small can sliced black olives
1 onion, chopped	8 ounces sharp Cheddar cheese,
2½ cups chunky salsa	shredded and divided
(hot or mild to taste)	8 large flour tortillas

- Brown meat and drain. Add onion and cook until transparent.
- Stir in ¾ cup salsa, olives and then 1 cup cheese.
- Spread 1¼ cups salsa into sprayed 9 x 13-inch baking dish.
- On each tortilla, place ¼ to ½ cup meat mixture, leaving room at each end.
- Roll up each tortilla, tuck in ends and place closely together seam side down on top of salsa.
- Top with remaining salsa, then remaining cheese.
- Bake at 350° for 20 minutes or until thoroughly heated.

Yield: 8 servings

For chicken enchiladas, substitute 2 cooked, skinned and boneless chicken breast halves, sliced into thin strips.

Taganini

1	(12-ounce) package noodles	2	(8-ounce) cans tomato sauce
1½	pounds ground beef	1	(10¾-ounce) can tomato soup
1	medium onion, chopped	¾	pound sharp Cheddar cheese,
2	tablespoons oil		grated, reserve ½ cup
	Salt and pepper to taste		Black olives, sliced
1	(15-ounce) can white corn,		
	drained		

- Cook noodles according to directions.
- Brown beef and onion in oil. Add salt and pepper.
- Combine corn, tomato sauce, soup, noodles and ½ cup cheese.
- Add beef and onions, mix well.
- Put in greased 9 x 13-inch casserole and top with remaining cheese.
- Bake at 350° for 45 minutes. Garnish with olives.

Yield: 10 to 12 servings

Miss Mary's Spaghetti Sauce

2	pounds ground round beef	2	bay leaves
2	tablespoons olive oil	1	tablespoon salt
4	(16-ounce) cans whole	1	clove garlic, minced
	tomatoes	2	tablespoons sugar
2	(12-ounce) cans tomato paste		Dash oregano
2	(12-ounce) cans water		Spaghetti

- Brown beef in olive oil in large heavy saucepan.
- Mix all other ingredients together, except spaghetti, while meat is cooking.
- Drain meat and add sauce mixture.
- Bring to a boil, reduce heat and simmer for 2 hours minimum.
- Serve over spaghetti.

Yield: 8 to 10 servings

Artichoke and Asparagus Strata

A great vegetarian main dish.

2	cups diced stale bread	1	cup chopped asparagus
2	cups shredded provolone or Swiss cheese, divided	6	eggs, beaten
		¼	cup white wine
1	leek, sliced thin	1½	cups milk
1½	cups sliced fresh mushrooms		Salt and pepper
1	cup artichoke hearts, drained and chopped	1	tablespoon fresh herbs

- Butter a 9 x 13-inch baking pan.

- Place bread in pan and sprinkle with ⅓ of the cheese.

- Sauté leeks in skillet until soft. Add mushrooms, artichokes and asparagus. Sauté until heated.

- Spread vegetable mixture over bread and cheese.

- Sprinkle with remaining cheese.

- Mix together eggs, wine, milk, salt, pepper and herbs. Pour over cheese.

- Shake pan so that liquids soak to bottom. Bake at 350° for 1 hour.

Yield: 6 to 8 servings

Stuffed Cabbage Rolls

1	pound lean ground beef	2	(8-ounce) cans tomato sauce
1	teaspoon salt	12	cabbage leaves, parboiled
¾	cup cooked rice	¼	cup brown sugar
1	small onion, chopped	¼	cup lemon juice

- Combine first 4 ingredients with 1 can tomato sauce.
- Place equal parts of meat mixture on each leaf.
- Roll up leaves, turning edges in.
- Place rolls, seam side down in a greased 9 x 13-inch pan.
- Mix remaining can of tomato sauce with brown sugar and lemon juice.
- Pour over cabbage rolls, cover and bake at 350° for 1 hour.

Yield: 4 servings

Fancy Skillet Scallops

1½	pounds scallops	½-1	stick butter or margarine
¾	cup flour, seasoned with salt and pepper	⅓-½	cup white wine
		¾	cup grated Swiss cheese

- Shake scallops in seasoned flour.
- In a skillet, melt butter over medium high heat.
- Add scallops and as they begin to get brown bits, stir with spatula for several minutes.
- When you have white meat of scallop with a good amount of brown, add wine. Allow to bubble and almost cook away.
- Remove skillet from heat and sprinkle with cheese.
- Bring to table and serve from skillet.

Yield: 4 to 5 servings

Puttanesca Sauce for Pasta

A vegetarian main dish that's great for Lenten suppers.

2	tablespoons olive oil	1	can black olives (preferably
1	tablespoon chopped garlic		Kalamata, drained)
10	cloves garlic, roasted	1	tablespoon capers
½	green pepper, diced	½	teaspoon basil
1	medium onion, diced	½	teaspoon oregano
1	tablespoon minced shallot	½	teaspoon Italian seasoning
2	anchovies, minced	½	teaspoon thyme
½	cup clam juice	1	tablespoon brown sugar
½	cup Marsala wine		Pasta (Penne or other big pasta)
1	cup chopped tomatoes		Parmesan cheese
1	can tomato puree		

- In a heavy saucepan, sauté first 7 ingredients in oil until onions are translucent.

- Add remaining ingredients and bring to a boil.

- Reduce heat to simmer and continue simmering until reduced to desired thickness.

- Serve over pasta and pass freshly grated Parmesan cheese.

Yield: 3 cups or 6 (½-cup) servings

Shrimp and Scallops with Pasta

1	(7-ounce) small shell pasta	½	teaspoon cayenne pepper
⅓	cup butter or margarine	½	teaspoon dry mustard
¾	cup chopped green pepper	1	teaspoon Worcestershire sauce
¾	cup chopped onion	1	tablespoon white wine or brandy
¾	cup chopped celery	1	(4-ounce) can mushrooms
1	pound scallops	¾	pound shrimp, boiled and peeled
⅓	cup flour	1½	cups grated sharp Cheddar
1⅓	cups milk		cheese
1	teaspoon salt	1½	cups buttered bread crumbs

- Cook pasta by directions and drain.
- Melt butter in large skillet. Sauté green pepper, onion and celery.
- Add scallops and sauté until white.
- Add flour and stir to mix. Add milk slowly, stirring until smooth.
- Add salt, pepper, dry mustard, Worcestershire sauce and wine. Blend well and add mushrooms.
- Add shrimp and adjust flour or milk for desired consistency.
- Spray 9 x 13-inch baking dish with cooking spray.
- Layer ½ of each: pasta, seafood mixture, cheese. Repeat.
- Top with buttered crumbs and bake at 350° for 30 to 40 minutes or until bubbly and browned.

Yield: 8 to 10 servings

Dressed Up Poached Fish

1½ cups water	4 fillets of white fish such as
½ cup white wine	trout, flounder, grouper
¼ cup mixed chopped celery tops,	Parmesan cheese
minced onion and thinly	Paprika
sliced carrots	Lemon slices

- Mix water, wine and vegetables in large skillet with cover and bring to boil.
- Reduce to simmer. Slide in fish and cover.
- Cook for 5 minutes or until fish flakes easily.
- Remove with spatula and place on cookie sheet covered with foil and sprayed with cooking spray.
- Sprinkle with Parmesan cheese.
- Place under broiler until fish are bubbly and browned.
- Remove to serving platter and sprinkle with paprika and parsley. Garnish with lemon slices.

Yield: 4 servings

Baked Fish

1 (2½ to 3-pound) whole fresh	1 celery stalk, chopped
fish (trout, bass or blue fish)	2-3 slices bacon
2-3 parsley sprigs, cut up	Lemon wedges
2-3 slices onion	Tartar sauce

- Have fish dressed in round.
- Line baking dish with foil and coat with oil or cooking spray.
- Stuff cavity of fish with vegetables. Place bacon on top of fish.
- Bake at 400° for about 20 minutes or until opaque and flaky.
- Serve with lemon wedges and tartar sauce.

Yield: 4 servings

Easy Baked Fish Fillets

5	tablespoons butter	2	tablespoons grated Parmesan cheese
2	cloves garlic, minced		
1	ripe tomato, peeled, seeded and chopped	2	tablespoons chopped basil
		2	pounds fish fillets (like flounder)

- In a saucepan, heat 4 tablespoons butter until bubbly.
- Add garlic and tomato and cook 30 seconds.
- Remove from heat and while stirring, add cheese and basil.
- Lay fish fillets on flat surface.
- Spread half of each fillet with butter and cheese mixture.
- Fold over other half of fillet.
- Place in buttered baking dish and dot with remaining butter.
- Bake at 375° for 15 minutes. Pan juices may be poured over fish.

Yield: 4 servings

Down East Grilled Fish

	Juice of 1 lemon	1	clove garlic, crushed or minced
1	tablespoon soy sauce	2	pounds fish fillets - blues,
1	teaspoon Worcestershire sauce		Spanish, flounder, etc.
2	tablespoons olive oil or melted butter		Lemon slices
			Fresh parsley

- Combine lemon juice, soy sauce, Worcestershire sauce, oil and garlic in glass rectangular dish and mix well.
- Add fish to marinade and leave at room temperature 30 to 40 minutes, turning 3 times.
- To grill, use grilling basket for best results.
- Grill 5 minutes on each side or until fish is flaky.
- Serve immediately; garnish with lemon and parsley.

Yield: 6 to 8 servings

Beaufort Baked Flounder

1	(2 to 5-pound) dressed flounder	5-6 strips bacon
	Flour	Water to cover - approximately
	Salt and pepper to taste	2 cups
6	white potatoes, sliced thin	Ketchup (optional)
1	large onion, sliced thin	

- Place flounder in baking dish or roasting pan with black skin up.
- Score 2 to 3 times depending on fish size.
- Sprinkle lightly with flour, salt and pepper.
- Spread potatoes and onions around fish.
- Place bacon on top of fish, add ketchup if desired.
- Add water to barely cover vegetables and fish.
- Cover loosely with foil and bake at 400° for 30 minutes.
- Check for doneness. Fish will be white and flaky and vegetables tender.
- May require additional cooking for 15 to 20 minutes.

Yield: depends on size of flounder!

Crabmeat Casserole

1	small onion, finely chopped	½	teaspoon pepper
1	green pepper, chopped finely	1	tablespoon Worcestershire
	Butter		sauce
1	pound backfin crabmeat	1	tablespoon dry mustard
1	teaspoon salt	5	tablespoons mayonnaise

- Sauté onion and green pepper in butter, add to crabmeat.
- Add remaining ingredients and mix tenderly.
- Pour into buttered 8 x 8-inch baking dish and bake at 350° approximately 30 minutes.

Yield: 4 servings

Nancy's Crab Stuffed Potatoes

4	baking potatoes	1	cup grated sharp Cheddar cheese, divided
½	cup margarine		
½	cup skim milk	½	cup grated Swiss cheese
1	teaspoon salt	½-1	pound crabmeat
¼	teaspoon pepper		Paprika
4	teaspoons grated onion		Parsley

- Bake potatoes at 450° until soft, about 1 hour.
- Scoop out insides of potatoes and mash with margarine, milk, salt, pepper and onion.
- Save potato shells.
- Mix in ½ cup Cheddar cheese and all of Swiss cheese. Fold in crabmeat.
- Refill shells with potato mixture.
- Sprinkle with remaining Cheddar cheese, paprika and parsley.
- Bake at 400° for 15 minutes.

Yield: 8 servings

Crabmeat Quiche

1	(9-inch) deep dish pie crust	½	cup mayonnaise
6	ounces lump crabmeat	2	eggs
4	mushrooms, sliced	2	tablespoons flour
⅓	cup chopped scallions or green onions	½	cup milk
		1	teaspoon salt
4	ounces Swiss cheese, sliced		Pepper

- Arrange crabmeat in bottom of pie crust.
- Sprinkle mushrooms and onion over crabmeat, add cheese.
- Beat together mayonnaise, eggs, flour, milk, salt and pepper and pour over crab mixture.
- Bake at 350° for 40 minutes. Allow to cool until firm before serving.

Yield: 6 servings

"Beaufort Grocery Co." Crab Cakes

1	pound crabmeat (picked)	⅛	teaspoon white pepper
¼	cup finely chopped onion	½	teaspoon salt
1	egg	1	teaspoon chopped parsley
2	tablespoons dry sherry		Bread crumbs
¾	cup mayonnaise		Butter or oil
1	cup bread crumbs		

- Mix first 9 ingredients gently by hand.
- Form into 1¾ to 2-ounce patties. Dredge in more bread crumbs.
- Cook in medium hot skillet with butter or oil until brown on both sides.

Yield: 6 to 8 servings

Freezes well.

Elegant Crab Quiche

A great brunch dish!

1½	cups shredded sharp Cheddar cheese	½	cup chopped green onions
2	tablespoons flour	½	teaspoon salt
1¼	cups half-and-half milk		Dash pepper
4	eggs, beaten	1	(10-inch) unbaked deep dish
6	ounces backfin or lump crabmeat		pie crust

- Preheat oven to 350°.
- Toss cheese with flour.
- Add milk, eggs, crabmeat, onions and seasonings.
- Mix well and pour into pie crust.
- Bake at 350° for 55 to 60 minutes or until set.

Yield: 6 to 8 servings

Baked Crabmeat En Casserole

1 pound fresh crabmeat	1 teaspoon lemon juice
1 cup herb stuffing mix	1 teaspoon cayenne pepper
Milk	½ teaspoon salt
4 hard-boiled eggs, chopped	Bread crumbs
1 cup mayonnaise	Butter
1 teaspoon Worcestershire sauce	

- Pick over crabmeat to remove any shell.
- Put dry stuffing in measuring cup and add milk over stuffing to 1 cup line.
- Mix stuffing and milk with next 6 ingredients and gently add crabmeat.
- Pour into greased 2-quart casserole, top with bread crumbs and dot with butter.
- Bake at 350° for 20 to 30 minutes.

Yield: 8 servings

Can substitute 1 pound shrimp for crab or mix ½ pound crab and ½ pound shrimp.

Sautéed Soft Shell Crabs

6 soft-shell crabs	¼ teaspoon paprika
1 egg	½ cup packaged dry bread crumbs
¼ teaspoon pepper	¼ cup all-purpose flour
¼ teaspoon salt (optional)	½ cup butter or margarine

- Clean crabs, rinse well, dry with paper towels.
- Beat egg slightly with salt, pepper and paprika.
- Combine bread crumbs with flour.
- Dip crabs in egg mixture, then in crumb mixture, coating completely.
- Melt butter in large skillet and sauté crabs until crisp and golden, about 5 minutes each side.

Yield: 4 to 6 servings

"The Net House"
Stuffed Soft-Shell Crabs

1	celery stalk, chopped fine	1	pound backfin crabmeat,
1	tablespoon chopped onion		picked over
	(optional)	6	soft-shell crabs, cleaned
1	tablespoon chopped bell pepper		Buttermilk
¼	cup butter		Flour
½	cup crushed saltine crackers		Salt and pepper
½	teaspoon celery salt		Peanut oil
½	teaspoon seafood seasoning		Butter
1	pint milk		Fresh lemon juice
1	egg, beaten		Chopped dill

- Sauté celery, onion and green pepper in butter until soft.
- Mix cracker crumbs with celery salt and seafood seasoning.
- Warm milk slightly in microwave.
- Combine milk, sautéed vegetables and crumb mixture; add egg and crabmeat.
- Chill before using.
- Lift top shell of crab and stuff with ⅙ of crab mixture; gently cover mixture with top shell.
- Dip crab in buttermilk, then in flour seasoned with salt and pepper.
- Deep fry in peanut oil until crab floats; turn once more until done.
- Drain on a rack.
- Mix butter, lemon juice and dill to make lemon dill butter and serve with crabs.

Yield: 4 to 6 servings

Richard's Shrimp with Parsley Rice

1¾ cups chicken broth
1 cup rice
2 tablespoons butter
1 tablespoon olive oil
6-8 scallions, minced
5 cloves garlic, minced or crushed
1 pound large shrimp, peeled and deveined

4-6 tablespoons lemon juice
¼ teaspoon pepper
½ cup freshly grated Parmesan or Romano cheese
2 tablespoon chopped fresh parsley
Lemon slices

- In a saucepan, bring broth to a boil.
- Add rice, cover and simmer until done about 15 to 20 minutes. Set aside.
- Heat butter and oil in large skillet until hot but not smoky.
- Sauté scallions and garlic until softened. Add shrimp and cook until pink.
- Stir in lemon juice and pepper. Cook about 4 minutes longer.
- Stir the cheese and parsley into cooked rice and transfer to serving platter.
- Spoon shrimp mixture on top of rice and garnish with lemon slices.

Yield: 4 servings

Creamy Shrimp Pesto
with Fresh Angel Hair Pasta
Quick, easy and delicious!

1	pound medium shrimp, peeled and deveined	½	pint whipping cream
2	tablespoons butter	2-3	cloves garlic, minced
1	package Knorr's Pesto sauce	1	package angel hair pasta, fresh
¼	cup olive oil		Fresh Parmesan cheese, grated

- Sauté shrimp in butter in large pan until cooked.

- Prepare Knorr's Pesto sauce in small saucepan with olive oil.

- Add rest of ingredients and simmer until cream sauce has thickened.

- While shrimp and cream sauce is simmering, cook angel hair pasta until al dente.

- Serve shrimp and sauce over pasta. Sprinkle with cheese.

Yield: 4 to 5 servings

Shrimp Creole

4	tablespoons butter or bacon grease	¼	teaspoon pepper
1	large onion, chopped	1	teaspoon sugar
1	green pepper, chopped	1	teaspoon chili powder
1	celery stalk, diced	1	tablespoon Worcestershire sauce
1	clove garlic, minced	2	bay leaves
1	tablespoon flour		Dash Tabasco sauce (optional)
2	(14-ounce) cans diced or crushed tomatoes with juice	1½	pounds shrimp, boiled and peeled, if large, cut in half
1	teaspoon salt	2	cups cooked rice

- Sauté onion, pepper and celery in butter or bacon grease in heavy skillet.
- Add garlic and cook 1 minute.
- Add flour and blend into vegetables until dissolved and brown.
- Add tomatoes slowly, blending well and stirring until thickened.
- Add spices and simmer 10 to 15 minutes.
- If sauce becomes too thick, add 1 to 2 tablespoons water or white wine.
- Add shrimp and heat thoroughly, about 5 to 10 minutes; remove bay leaves.
- Serve over cooked rice.

Yield: 4 to 6 servings

Shrimp and Snow Peas Stir-Fry

1 pound fresh shrimp, peeled and deveined	2 tablespoons sesame oil
1 teaspoon salt	3-5 slices fresh ginger
2 teaspoons corn starch	1 cup snow peas
2 teaspoons sherry	¼ cup chicken stock
2 scallions	Salt and pepper
1 tablespoon peanut oil	2 tablespoons sesame seeds, toasted

- Place shrimp in bowl with salt, cornstarch and sherry. Mix well and set aside.
- Cut scallions in ½ lengthwise and crosswise in 1-inch lengths.
- Heat sauté pan or large skillet, add oils and swirl to cover sides.
- Add ginger and toss a few seconds.
- Add peas, scallions and chicken stock and cover, steaming 30 to 40 seconds.
- Add shrimp and toss constantly until they turn pink, 1 to 2 minutes.
- Season to taste and sprinkle with sesame seeds.

Yield: 4 servings

Sugar snaps can be substituted for snow peas.

Shrimp Linguine

1	pound linguine	1	small yellow onion, chopped
1	cup chicken broth	2	cloves garlic, minced
2	tablespoons lemon juice	1	teaspoon tomato paste
1	bay leaf	2	tablespoons chopped fresh
1	pound shrimp, peeled and		basil
	deveined	½	teaspoon black pepper
1	tablespoon olive oil		

- Cook linguine according to directions but do not add salt.
- In a large skillet, combine broth, lemon juice and bay leaf. Bring to a boil over medium heat.
- Add shrimp, cover and cook until shrimp turn pink, about 2 minutes.
- Remove shrimp, reserving liquid; cover to keep warm.
- In same skillet, heat oil over medium heat and add onion, garlic and tomato paste. Cook for 5 minutes, stirring frequently.
- Add reserved liquid, basil and pepper and cook until thickened, about 3 minutes; remove bay leaf.
- Add shrimp to skillet and cook, stirring constantly, until heated, about 1 minute.
- Pour over linguine and serve immediately.

Yield: 6 servings

V's Shrimp Casserole

2	pounds cooked shrimp, diced	1	medium onion, diced or 1
3-4	slices soft bread, cubed		tablespoon dry minced onion
1-1¼	cups evaporated milk	⅛	teaspoon pepper
1¼	cups mayonnaise	2	tablespoons sherry
3	large eggs, hard-boiled and	1	tablespoon Accent
	chopped	2	dashes of red pepper flakes
3	tablespoons minced fresh		Salt and pepper to taste
	parsley or 1 tablespoon dry	½	cup herb seasoned stuffing mix
	parsley		Butter

- Cook shrimp 2 to 3 minutes in boiling water until pink.
- Soak bread in milk while peeling and dicing shrimp.
- Add all other ingredients except stuffing mix to bread; fold in shrimp.
- Place in greased 9 x 13-inch casserole. If not serving immediately, refrigerate at this point and remove 20 minutes before baking.
- Sprinkle with stuffing mix and dot with butter.
- Bake at 350° for 30 minutes or until browned.

Yield: 8 servings

For a delicious variation, reduce shrimp to 1 pound and add 1 pound crabmeat.

Barbecued Shrimp

3	slices bacon, chopped	1	teaspoon fresh ground black
½	pound butter or margarine		pepper
2	tablespoons Dijon mustard	½	teaspoon oregano
1½	tablespoons chili powder	2	cloves garlic, crushed
¼	teaspoon basil	2	tablespoons seafood seasoning
¼	teaspoon thyme	½	teaspoon Tabasco sauce
		1½	pounds large shrimp with shells

- In small frying pan, fry bacon just until clear.

- Add the butter and all other ingredients except the shrimp. Simmer 5 minutes.

- Place shrimp in open baking dish and pour sauce over top. Stir once to coat.

- Bake uncovered at 375° for about 20 minutes, depending on size and amount of shrimp. Stir twice during baking process.

- Transfer to a clean casserole dish to stop cooking process (optional). Serve immediately!

Yield: 6 servings

You may peel these shrimp before eating, but not before cooking. Some people eat them shells and all. Have a damp towel for each guest because this most delicious dish is very messy.

Grilled Shrimp

1½	pounds fresh uncooked shrimp, peeled and deveined	⅛	teaspoon oregano
¾	cup salad oil	⅛	teaspoon basil
1	medium onion, grated	⅛	teaspoon ground cloves
2	tablespoons lemon juice	½	teaspoon celery seed
1	clove garlic, finely chopped	½	teaspoon chili powder
		½	teaspoon salt

- Combine all ingredients.
- Marinate in refrigerator for 1 to 3 hours.
- Place shrimp on skewers.
- Grill over charcoal for 3 minutes on each side.

Yield: 4 to 6 servings

May be served as a Main Course or Appetizer.

Seafood Alfredo

1½	cups water	1	pound imitation crab, lobster, crabmeat, or shrimp, peeled and cooked
1	cup sliced carrots		
½	cup milk		
1	cup chopped broccoli	¼-⅓	cup sliced almonds
1	package Noodles Alfredo		

- Simmer carrots in water 5 minutes in large saucepan.
- Add milk, broccoli and noodle mix, cover and simmer 5 more minutes stirring occasionally.
- Add seafood, sprinkle almonds on top, cover and cook gently for another 5 minutes.
- Add more water or milk if too dry. Adjust seasoning if desired.
- Serve in large pasta bowl.

Yield: 6 servings

"The Net House"
Shrimp Quiche

2	(9-inch) deep dish pie crusts	1	cup grated sharp Cheddar cheese
	Egg white	3	cups heavy cream
½	pound shrimp, peeled and	6	eggs
	deveined, boiled until barely	3	tablespoons flour
	pink	¼	teaspoon cayenne pepper
⅔	cup chopped green onion	¼	teaspoon nutmeg
1	cup grated Swiss cheese		Pinch of salt

- Pierce sides and bottom of crusts thoroughly with fork.

- Bake at 400° for 7 minutes. Brush with egg whites. Set aside.

- Mix shrimp, onion and cheeses. Divide and sprinkle evenly into pie crusts.

- Whip together cream, eggs, flour, cayenne, nutmeg and salt; strain through a mesh strainer (this ensures no clumps of flour).

- Divide and pour over filling in crusts.

- Bake on a cookie sheet on bottom oven rack at 375° for 35 to 45 minutes.

- Test with knife. Cover outer ring of crust with foil as it may become too done.

- Quiche needs to cool completely in order to set up firmly.

Yield: 6 to 8 servings

To freeze, wait until set, cover with plastic wrap and then foil or place in zip lock. To reheat, thaw completely, slice into portion and microwave on medium heat until desired temperature.

Fried Menhaden Roe

Carteret County caviar!

1 pint to 1 quart menhaden roe Salt and pepper to taste Flour or cornmeal	Bacon grease or corn oil - enough to cover bottom of frying pan

- Wash roe thoroughly removing all black parts.

- Place on wax paper and separate into single pieces.

- Sprinkle with salt and pepper and dredge in flour or cornmeal to completely coat.

- In a heavy skillet, fry in bacon grease or oil over medium heat until golden brown; may need to cover pan to prevent popping. Can also be deep fat fried.

Yield: depend on appetites

A coastal breakfast dish with pancakes and cheese grits or a Sunday supper delicacy with hash browns, slaw and cornbread.

Scalloped Oysters

1	pint fresh oysters	¾	cup light cream
2	cups saltine cracker crumbs (46 crackers)	¼	teaspoon Worcestershire sauce
		½	teaspoon salt
½	cup butter, melted	¼	teaspoon pepper
1	cup sliced mushrooms, fresh or bottled	2	tablespoons parsley flakes

- Drain oysters, reserving ¼ cup liquid.

- Combine crumbs and melted butter. Set aside ½ cup crumbs.

- Combine remaining crumbs with oysters, liquid, mushrooms, cream, Worcestershire sauce and seasonings.

- Turn into 2-quart baking dish. Top with reserved crumbs.

- Bake at 350° for 40 minutes.

Yield: 4 to 6 servings

Desserts

Gentlemen Strollers - Watercolor

Richard Meelheim

Mr. Meelheim is a resident of Beaufort and a member of
St. Paul's. He began drawing and painting in the 1980's. Mostly
self-taught, he also attended workshops and short courses led
by artists such as Charles Sharpe. His work is shown in
invitational shows and several local galleries.

Miss Matt's Lemon Meringue Pie

5	tablespoons cornstarch	5	tablespoons lemon juice
2	cups water	3	teaspoons grated lemon rind
1	cup sugar	1	(9-inch) pie crust, baked
¼	teaspoon salt	3	egg whites
2	egg yolks, slightly beaten	6	tablespoons sugar
2	tablespoons butter		

- Mix cornstarch with ½ cup of the water in the top of a double boiler; blend in sugar and salt.
- Add remainder of water until well blended.
- Cook over low heat, stirring constantly, until mixture boils.
- Cover and continue to cook over boiling water for 10 minutes.
- Gradually pour hot mixture over egg yolks, stirring constantly.
- Return to double boiler and cook 2 minutes.
- Remove from heat, add butter, lemon juice and lemon rind.
- Mix well, cool and pour into pie crust.
- For meringue-beat egg whites until stiff, gradually add sugar.
- Cover lemon filling, sealing meringue to edges of pie crust.
- Bake at 350° until lightly browned.

Yield: 6 to 8 servings

Extra Elegant Apple Pie

Filling

2	tablespoons flour
½	teaspoon salt
¾	cup sugar
1	egg, beaten
1	cup sour cream

½	teaspoon vanilla
2	cups finely chopped apples (Granny Smith or Tart Red)
1	(9-inch) unbaked pie crust

Topping

⅓	cup plain flour
⅓	cup sugar
	Dash salt

1	teaspoon cinnamon
¼	cup butter, melted

- Sift together flour, salt and sugar.
- Add egg, sour cream and vanilla and beat well.
- Stir in apples. Pour into pie crust.
- Bake at 425° for 15 minutes.
- Reduce heat to 350° and bake 30 minutes.
- Combine all topping ingredients and mix well.
- Remove pie from oven, sprinkle on topping; return to 400° oven for 10 minutes.

Yield: 6 to 8 servings

Apple Chess Pie

1¼ cups peeled and grated apples
1¼ cups sugar
2   tablespoons flour
1   egg
½   stick butter, melted

1   teaspoon vanilla extract
¼   teaspoon cinnamon
¼   teaspoon nutmeg
1   (9-inch) unbaked pie crust

- Preheat oven to 450°.
- Mix all ingredients together and pour into unbaked pie crust.
- Bake 10 minutes at 450°.
- Turn oven back to 350° and bake 30 minutes.

Yield: 6 servings

Fresh Peach Pie

1   cup sugar
2   tablespoons flour
2   large eggs
2   tablespoons butter, softened

Pinch nutmeg
1½   pounds peaches, peeled and
     sliced
1   (9-inch) unbaked pie crust

- Preheat oven to 350°.
- Whisk together sugar, flour, eggs, butter and nutmeg.
- Arrange peaches in pie crust.
- Pour mixture over peaches.
- Bake in middle of oven 50 to 55 minutes or until just set.
- Cool completely before serving.
- Serve with ice cream, if desired.

Yield: 6 to 8 servings

Fresh Peach or Nectarine Tart

1	unbaked refrigerated pie crust	1	teaspoon vanilla
⅓	cup finely chopped nuts	½	teaspoon cinnamon
4-6	peaches or nectarines	½	teaspoon nutmeg
	(1 very ripe)	2	heaping tablespoons cornstarch
1	cup water	1	tablespoon cold water
1	tablespoon lemon juice	½	teaspoon almond extract
½	cup sugar		Whipped cream or topping
2	tablespoons sugar		
1	(8-ounce) package cream cheese, softened		

- Press crust into tart pan, press nuts into crust and prick closely.
- Bake at 325° until brown, about 20 minutes.
- Remove to rack and cool completely.
- Chop the 1 ripe peach or nectarine into fine pieces and add water, lemon juice and ½ cup sugar in saucepan.
- Simmer 10 minutes, cool and then strain out the largest pieces and discard.
- Mix 2 tablespoons sugar, cream cheese, vanilla, cinnamon and nutmeg.
- Spread on bottom and sides of tart shell, refrigerate.
- Return fruit mixture to medium heat and add cornstarch mixed with 1 tablespoon cold water, stir until thickened and clear.
- Remove from heat; add almond extract and dash of nutmeg, cool.
- Slice remaining peaches or nectarines and place in circles over cream cheese until completely covered.
- Cover fruit with cornstarch mixture, pipe whipped cream or topping around edge, chill.

Yield: 8 servings

Aunt Sallie's Blueberry Cream Pie

1	(9-inch) deep dish unbaked pie crust	1	(8-ounce) package cream cheese, softened
1	quart blueberries	2	tablespoons cream
1	cup sugar	2	tablespoons powdered sugar
3	tablespoons minute tapioca	2	cups sweetened whipped cream
3	tablespoons flour	1	teaspoon vanilla
6-7	pats butter		

- Put berries in pie crust.
- Mix sugar, tapioca and flour.
- Sprinkle over berries, lifting to cover all; dot with butter.
- Bake at 375° for 40 to 45 minutes. Cool.
- For the topping, mix cream cheese with cream and powdered sugar.
- Fold into whipped cream and vanilla.
- Spread over cooled filling and refrigerate.

Yield: 6 to 8 servings

Cranberry and Raisin Pie

2	cups cranberries	1½	tablespoons flour
½	cup raisins	1	cup chopped walnuts
¾	cup sugar	1	(9-inch) unbaked pie crust
½	cup water	1	extra crust for lattice top

- Mix together berries, raisins, sugar, water and flour.
- Cook in saucepan 10 minutes.
- Add walnuts and pour into pie shell.
- Cover with lattice crust.
- Bake at 425° for 10 minutes, then reduce to 350° for 30 minutes.
- Serve with vanilla ice cream or hard sauce.

Yield: 6 to 8 servings

Holiday Cranberry Surprise Pie

A real treat when cranberries are in season!

2	cups fresh cranberries	2	eggs, beaten
½	cup sugar	¾	cup butter or margarine, melted
½	cup pecans or walnuts	1	cup self-rising flour
1	cup sugar		

- Grease 10-inch pie plate.
- Spread cranberries on bottom.
- Sprinkle sugar and nuts over cranberries.
- In a mixing bowl combine sugar, eggs and melted butter.
- Add flour to mixture and stir well. Pour over cranberries.
- Bake at 320° for 60 minutes or until crust is golden brown.

Yield: 8 servings

Delicious served warm with whipped cream or ice cream.

Easy Coconut Pie

Quick and easy - makes its own crust!

4	eggs	¼	cup butter, melted
1¾	cups sugar	1½	cups coconut
½	cup self-rising flour	1	teaspoon vanilla or lemon
2	cups milk		flavoring

- Combine all ingredients in order and mix well.
- Pour into greased 10-inch pie plate and bake at 350° for 45 minutes or until golden brown.

Yield: 6 to 8 servings

Irene's Coconut Pie

4	eggs	1	stick margarine, melted
1½	cups sugar	1	teaspoon vanilla
2	cups flaked coconut	2	(9-inch) unbaked pie crusts
1	cup buttermilk		

- Preheat oven to 350°.
- Beat eggs by hand until fluffy. Add sugar while beating eggs.
- Add remaining ingredients.
- Pour into 2 unbaked pie crusts.
- Bake at 350° for 45 minutes.

Yield: 2 pies

Summer Pecan Pie

3	egg whites	2	cups pecans, finely chopped
1	cup sugar	1	teaspoon vanilla
10	saltine crackers, crushed		

- Beat egg whites until stiff but not dry.
- Beat in sugar.
- Fold in other ingredients, stirring gently.
- Bake in greased 9-inch pie pan at 350° for 30 to 35 minutes.

Yield: 8 servings

Makes its own crust!

Pecan-Fruit Pie

1	stick margarine, melted	½	cup chopped pecans
2	eggs, slightly beaten	1	teaspoon vanilla
1	cup sugar		Dash salt
½	cup flaked coconut	1	(9-inch) unbaked pie crust
½	cup raisins		

- Mix all ingredients in large mixing bowl.
- Pour into pie crust and bake at 350° for 30 minutes.
- Let cool. May be refrigerated or served at room temperature.
- Serve plain or with vanilla ice cream.

Yield: 8 servings

Decadent Chocolate Chess Pie

1	stick margarine	1½	tablespoons milk
1½	squares unsweetened chocolate	1	teaspoon vanilla
1	cup brown sugar	1	(9-inch) unbaked pie crust
½	cup white sugar	1	(8-ounce) carton whipped
1½	tablespoons flour		topping
	Dash salt	½	cup nuts, toasted
2	eggs, beaten with fork	1	bar sweet chocolate

- Melt margarine and chocolate over low heat.
- Add sugars, flour, salt, eggs, milk and vanilla, mix thoroughly.
- Pour into pie crust and bake at 325° for 35 to 45 minutes, or until it puffs up and splits slightly on top. Cool completely.
- Serve covered with whipped topping, sprinkle with nuts.
- Use a vegetable peeler to make chocolate curls to decorate top.

Yield: 8 servings

May be made 2 days ahead, refrigerated and then decorated to serve. Very rich!

Billy's Chocolate Meringue Pie

1   (9-inch) Ritz cracker, graham
    cracker or regular pie crust

Cracker Crust
30-36   Ritz crackers   2   tablespoons butter

*   Crush 18 crackers and mix with butter.
*   Pat in bottom of 9-inch pie plate.
*   Stand up remaining whole crackers around edge of pie plate.
*   Refrigerate until well chilled.

Filling
2   heaping tablespoons flour   2   egg yolks, slightly beaten
2   heaping tablespoons cocoa   4   tablespoons butter
1   cup sugar   1   teaspoon vanilla
2   cups evaporated milk

*   Mix dry ingredients well, add milk and egg yolks.
*   Bring to a boil in heavy saucepan over medium heat, stirring frequently until it comes to full rolling boil.
*   Remove from heat and add butter and vanilla, mix well.
*   Let cool for 5 minutes, stirring twice.
*   Pour into pie crust, top with meringue and bake at 400° until brown.

Meringue
3   egg whites, room temperature   ½   teaspoon vanilla
¼   teaspoon cream of tartar   6   tablespoons sugar

*   Beat egg whites and cream of tartar until soft peak form.
*   Add vanilla and sugar, continuing to beat until stiff peak form.

Yield: 6 to 8 servings

Caribbean Fudge Pie

1	(12-ounce) package semi-sweet chocolate pieces	¼	cup butter, melted
¾	cup sugar	3	eggs
2	teaspoons brewed coffee	1½	cups chopped nuts, divided
1	teaspoon Tía Maria or almond extract	¼	cup flour
		1	(9-inch) unbaked pie crust
		½	cup nuts

- Melt chocolate over low heat or in microwave.
- Mix sugar, coffee and Tía Maria or almond extract, add butter.
- Beat in eggs 1 at a time.
- Add melted chocolate and mix well until smooth.
- Add 1 cup nuts and flour and mix well until smooth.
- Pour into pie crust and sprinkle with ½ cup nuts.
- Bake at 350° for 40 to 45 minutes, test for doneness.
- Let cool at least 2 hours to room temperature.
- Serve with whipped cream or vanilla ice cream.

Yield: 6 to 8 servings

Strawberry Daiquiri Pie

A quick and easy summer dessert.

1	(12-ounce) can frozen strawberry daiquiri mix, thawed	16	ounces whipped topping
1	can condensed milk	1	cup fresh or frozen strawberries, drained and chopped fine
1-2	tablespoons dry lemonade mix	2	graham cracker pie crusts

- Mix first 5 ingredients until well blended.
- Divide and pour into crusts and freeze at least 6 hours.

Yield: 2 pies

For lemonade or limeade pie, change strawberry mix to 1 can lemonade or limeade, thawed and omit strawberries.

Caramel Coconut Pie

2 (9-inch) pie crusts, baked	1 (14-ounce) can condensed milk
¼ cup butter	16 ounces whipped topping
1 (7-ounce) package coconut	1 (12-ounce) jar caramel ice
½ cup chopped pecans	cream topping
1 (8-ounce) package cream	Pecan halves (optional)
cheese, softened	

- Bake pie shells according to directions and cool.
- Melt butter in large skillet, add coconut and pecans.
- Cook until golden, stirring frequently. Set aside, cool slightly.
- Combine cream cheese and milk and beat at medium speed until smooth.
- Fold in whipped topping.
- Layer ¼ cream cheese mixture, ¼ caramel topping and ¼ coconut mixture on each pie. Repeat, then cover and freeze at least 8 hours.
- Let frozen pies stand at room temperature for 5 minutes before slicing.
- Garnish with whole pecans if desired.

Yield: 2 pies or 16 servings

Just Can't Fail Pie Crust

This crust is flaky and crispy, no matter what you do to it.

4 cups all-purpose flour	1 tablespoon vinegar
1 tablespoon sugar	1 egg
2 teaspoons salt	½ cup ice water
1¾ cups solid vegetable shortening	

- Put flour, sugar and salt in bowl, whisk to mix.
- Add shortening and cut in until mixture is crumbly and there are no big pieces of fat.
- In a small bowl, use a fork to combine vinegar, egg and water.
- Add flour and stir with fork until all ingredients are just moistened and dough forms a ball. Divide into ¼ or ⅕ amounts.
- Put what you plan to use in refrigerator for 30 minutes to chill.
- With remaining dough, make discs about 5 to 6 inches, wrap with clear wrap and put in zip freezer bag and tightly close, freeze.
- Roll out on well-floured pastry cloth.

Yield: 4 to 5 (9-inch) crusts

Dough will keep in freezer for 3 months - thaws in about 20 minutes.

Almond Pound Cake with Caramel Icing

Cake

3	sticks butter, softened
3	cups sugar, sifted
8	eggs

3	cups cake flour, sifted
1	teaspoon vanilla extract
1	teaspoon almond extract

- With mixer, beat butter until creamy.
- Add sugar and mix until combined.
- Add eggs 1 at a time, beating well after each addition.
- Add flour 1 cup at a time, beating well after each addition.
- Add vanilla and almond extracts and mix well.
- Pour into a greased and floured 10-inch tube pan.
- Bake at 300° for 1 hour and 20 minutes or until brown and crusty on top.
- Cool in pan on rack for 30 minutes and then remove from pan and cool completely before icing.

Caramel Icing

2	sticks butter
1	(1-pound) box light brown sugar
10	tablespoons canned evaporated milk

1	teaspoon vanilla
1	teaspoon baking powder

- Melt butter in medium saucepan on medium to medium low heat.
- Add brown sugar and evaporated milk.
- Mix well until mixture starts to boil, stirring constantly.
- Boil for 3 minutes, being sure to watch heat level and prevent scorching.
- Remove from heat and add vanilla and baking powder.
- Beat with electric mixer until icing starts to harden. The amount of time for this varies.
- Icing will continue to harden while applying to cake.

Yield: 10 to 12 servings

Jane D's Chocolate Pound Cake

Cake

3	sticks butter, softened	½	teaspoon salt
3	cups sugar	1	cup milk
5-6	eggs	½	teaspoon baking powder
3	cups flour	2	teaspoons vanilla
½	cup cocoa		

- Cream butter and sugar for 5 minutes.
- Add eggs 1 at a time, beating well after each.
- Combine flour, cocoa and salt in another bowl.
- Dissolve baking powder in milk, add vanilla.
- Add flour mixture and milk to butter, sugar and eggs, alternating but beginning and ending with flour, beating after each.
- Bake in a greased tube pan for 1½ hours at 320°.

No Cook Chocolate Icing

1	box powdered sugar	2	tablespoons milk
⅔	cup cocoa	1	teaspoon vanilla
1	stick butter, softened		Chopped nuts (optional)

- Mix sugar and cocoa, add butter; beat until well blended.
- Add milk and vanilla and beat well.
- Add more milk if necessary for spreading consistency.
- Top with chopped nuts, if desired.

Yield: 12 to 16 servings

Black Walnut Chocolate Pound Cake

2	sticks butter, softened	5	tablespoons cocoa
½	cup shortening	1	cup milk
3	cups sugar	1	teaspoon black walnut flavoring
5	eggs	1	square unsweetened chocolate,
3	cups plain flour		melted
½	teaspoon baking powder	½	cup chopped black walnuts
½	teaspoon salt		

- Preheat oven to 325°.
- Cream well butter, shortening and sugar.
- Beat in eggs 1 at a time.
- Sift together flour, baking powder, salt and cocoa.
- Add to creamed mixture, alternately with milk.
- Add flavoring and chocolate. Fold in nuts.
- Bake in well-greased and floured tube pan for 1 hour and 20 minutes.
- Do not open door during baking.

Yield: 12 to 14 servings

Fresh Peach Pound Cake

1 cup plus 2 tablespoons butter, softened	3 cups all-purpose flour, divided
2¼ cups sugar	1 teaspoon baking powder
4 eggs	½ teaspoon salt
½ teaspoon vanilla	2 cups chopped fresh peaches
½ teaspoon lemon flavoring	¼ teaspoon cinnamon
¼ teaspoon almond flavoring	¼ teaspoon nutmeg
	Dash ginger

- Grease tube pan with 2 tablespoons butter.

- Sprinkle pan with ¼ cup sugar.

- Cream remaining butter and gradually add remaining sugar; beat well.

- Add eggs 1 at a time, beating well after each.

- Add flavorings and mix well.

- Combine 2¾ cups flour, baking powder and salt.

- Gradually add to creamed mixture, beating until well blended.

- Dredge peaches with remaining ¼ cup flour, cinnamon, nutmeg and ginger; fold into batter.

- Pour into prepared pan and bake at 325° for 1 hour and 10 minutes.

- Remove from pan and cool completely.

Yield: 16 servings

Walnut Pound Cake

1	box yellow cake mix	4	eggs
1	(3-ounce) package instant	1	teaspoon walnut flavoring
	vanilla pudding	1	cup broken walnuts
1	cup water	1½	cups powdered sugar
⅓	cup oil		Water

- Mix cake mix, pudding mix, water and oil.
- Add eggs 1 at a time, mixing well after each.
- Add flavoring and nuts.
- Pour into a greased and floured tube pan.
- Bake at 350° for 50 minutes.
- Mix powdered sugar with enough water to make a creamy consistency.
- Remove cake from pan.
- While cake is still hot, spread glaze over cake.

Yield: 12 to 14 servings

Fresh Apple Nut Cake

3	eggs	1	teaspoon salt
2	cups sugar	1	teaspoon baking soda
1½	cups oil	1	teaspoon vanilla
3	cups diced and peeled apples	1	cup chopped pecans
3	cups flour		

- Mix eggs, sugar and oil.
- Add apples, flour, salt, soda, vanilla and chopped nuts and mix thoroughly.
- Pour into greased and floured 10-inch Bundt pan.
- Bake at 350° for 1 hour and 15 minutes.

Yield: 12 to 16 servings

Vanilla Pound Cake Loaves

1 cup solid shortening	2 teaspoons vanilla
2 sticks margarine, softened	3 cups flour
3 cups sugar	1 cup milk
5 eggs, room temperature	½ teaspoon baking powder

- Combine first 5 ingredients in large mixing bowl.
- Beat until mixture is consistency of whipping cream.
- Add 1 cup flour, mix well, add ½ cup milk, mix well, add 1 cup flour, mix well, add ½ cup milk, mix well, add 1 cup flour, mix well.
- Add baking powder and mix.
- Grease bottom of 2 loaf pans, then use wax paper in pan, turning paper once to distribute shortening.
- Bake 35 minutes at 325°, then 30 minutes at 350°.

Yield: 2 loaves

Blackberry Wine Cake

1 box white cake mix	1 cup blackberry wine
1 package blackberry gelatin	1 cup powdered sugar
4 eggs	¼ cup blackberry wine
1 cup oil	

- Mix cake mix, gelatin, eggs, oil and wine on low speed for 1 minute.
- Increase speed to medium high and beat for 3 minutes.
- Pour into greased and floured Bundt cake pan.
- Bake at 350° for 45 minutes.
- Combine powdered sugar and ¼ cup wine to make glaze.
- Turn cake out of pan and onto a cake rack over a tray.
- Make numerous holes on the top and sides with a cake tester.
- While still hot, pour glaze over top and sides.

Yield: 18 servings

The Point Spice Cake

1	cup oil	1	teaspoon cinnamon
2	cups sugar	1	teaspoon nutmeg
3	eggs	1	cup buttermilk
2	cups plain flour	½	cup applesauce
1	teaspoon salt	½	cup fig or pear preserves
1	teaspoon baking soda	1	cup chopped pecans
½	teaspoon cloves		

- Beat first 3 ingredients at medium speed until blended.
- Combine flour and next 5 ingredients.
- Add to mixture and beat until blended.
- Add last 5 ingredients and beat at medium speed for 2 minutes.
- Pour into greased and floured tube pan.
- Bake at 325° for 1 hour, reduce heat to 315° and cook for 10 minutes.
- Cool in pan 20 minutes, then invert onto plate.

Yield: 18 servings

"Pecan Tree Inn" Ginger Ale Cake

1	box Duncan Hines Lemon Supreme cake mix	½	cup ginger ale
3	eggs	½	cup sugar
1	(8-ounce) carton sour cream	2	teaspoons cinnamon
½	cup vegetable oil	1	cup chopped pecans
			Powdered sugar

• Preheat oven to 350°.

• Grease and flour a Bundt pan.

• Beat first 5 ingredients with an electric mixer for just 2 minutes.

• Fold in sugar, cinnamon and nuts.

• Pour into greased and floured pan.

• Bake at 350° for 55 to 60 minutes or until a toothpick comes out clean.

• Cool 20 minutes and remove.

• Sprinkle on powdered sugar just before serving.

Yield: 12 to 15 servings

Lasts for several days if refrigerated. Very moist.

Grand Marnier Cake

2   cups sugar
1   cup butter, softened
2   eggs
2   cups all-purpose flour, unsifted
½   teaspoon salt
1   teaspoon baking powder
1   cup sour cream
1   teaspoon vanilla

1   tablespoon Grand Mariner or
      orange juice
    Grated rind of 1 orange
1½ cups almonds, toasted
4   tablespoons butter, melted
⅓   cup Grand Marnier
    Powdered sugar

- Preheat oven to 350°.
- Cream sugar and butter thoroughly and blend in eggs.
- Sift dry ingredients and add alternately with sour cream, vanilla and Grand Marnier or juice; blend in orange rind.
- Pour ½ mixture in a well-greased and floured tube or Bundt pan.
- Add 1 cup almonds, then remaining cake mixture.
- Bake at 350° for 1 hour, cool on rack for 10 minutes.
- For a topping, melt butter and add Grand Marnier.
- Pierce entire top of cake and pour mixture over.
- Cool 30 minutes in pan; turn out onto plate.
- Sprinkle with remaining ½ cup almonds and powdered sugar.

Yield: 12 servings

Grand Marnier Apple Cake

1	cup golden raisins	1	teaspoon salt
	Grand Marnier	1	teaspoon cinnamon
1½	cups oil or ½ cup oil and 1 cup	1	teaspoon vanilla
	applesauce	1	teaspoon baking soda
2	cups sugar	1	cup chopped pecans or other
3	eggs		nuts, toasted
3	cups flour	3	cups small apple chunks

- Plump raisins - cover raisins with Grand Marnier for at least 24 hours.
- Beat oil and sugar together, add eggs, beating well.
- Sift flour, salt, cinnamon and baking soda together and add to creamed mixture; mix well.
- Add vanilla, then fold in nuts, raisins and apples.
- Pour into greased and floured tube pan or muffin tin.
- Bake at 350° for 1 hour and 15 minutes for cake; bake at 300° for 35 to 40 minutes for muffins.

Yield: 12 servings

Best made a day before serving. Plumped raisins can be stored in airtight container for many months.

Apple Cake Squares

3	cups peeled and chopped apples	2	teaspoons vanilla
2	cups sugar	3	cups flour, sifted
1½	cups vegetable oil	1	cup light brown sugar
3	eggs, well beaten	1	stick butter
1	teaspoon baking soda	1	teaspoon vanilla
1	teaspoon salt	¼	cup evaporated milk

- In a large mixing bowl, fold together apples, sugar and oil.

- Add eggs, soda, salt, vanilla and flour and mix well.

- Pour into greased 9 x 13-inch or 2 (8 x 8-inch) baking pans.

- Place in cold oven and set at 325° for 1 hour.

- While cake bakes, mix brown sugar, butter, vanilla and milk in a saucepan; bring to a good boil.

- Use a 2-prong fork to make holes over cake top.

- Pour icing over hot cake and leave in pan until ready to serve.

Yield: 18 squares

"Beaufort Grocery Co." Lemon Cheesecake

2½	cups graham cracker crumbs	3	cups sugar
¼	cup powdered sugar		Zest of 2 lemons
5	tablespoons butter, melted	10	eggs
3	pounds cream cheese, softened	¾	cup fresh squeezed lemon juice

- Preheat oven to 350°.
- In a large bowl, combine crumbs, powdered sugar and butter until well blended.
- Spray a 10-inch springform pan with nonstick vegetable spray and press crumb mixture evenly on the bottom.
- In a large mixing bowl, beat cream cheese until all lumps are gone and is smooth.
- Add sugar and lemon zest and beat well.
- On low speed, add eggs, 1 at a time until well blended.
- Stir in lemon juice.
- Pour batter into crust-filled pan.
- Bake at 350° for 1 hour and 30 minutes.
- Turn oven off and leave in until oven is cool.
- Refrigerate.

Yield: 18 servings

Bitsy's Favorite Fruitcake

Adapted from Aunt Maud Ramsey's recipe - an old Brooks family recipe.

10   ounces shortening
8   extra-large eggs
2   cups sugar
2½   cups raisins, plumped in ⅓ cup
     white wine
2½   cups flour
2   teaspoons baking powder
1   heaping teaspoon of each: salt,
     allspice, mace, cinnamon,
     nutmeg, cloves and ginger
2   cups flour for fruit and nuts

1¾   cups dates, cut up
1   quart plus ½ cup Fruit Cake mix
1   quart chopped pecans and
     walnuts
1   cup chopped almonds
1   cup diced apricots
1   cup diced prunes
1   cup dried cranberries
½   cup each wine and molasses
1   pint brandy

- Cream shortening, eggs and sugar.
- Mix with a whisk all dry ingredients.
- Flour all fruit and nuts with 2 cups flour.
- Add wine and molasses to creamed mixture.
- Beat into this mixture the flour and spices.
- Add floured fruit and nuts (a large roaster pan works), mix with a large spoon until all is coated.
- Bake in 10 (5¾ x 3 x 2-inch) greased pans or 2 tube pans at 275° until firm to touch.
- While warm and in pans, sprinkle with a good brandy.
- Cool in pans, sprinkle heavily with brandy.
- Repeat 4 more times over 3 or 4 days (will use the pint of brandy).
- Wrap tightly with cling wrap.

Yield: 10 small loaves or 2 tube loaves

Keeps well. Can be frozen or delicious fresh from oven.

Mocha Walnut Torte

1	brownie or chocolate cake recipe (2 pans)	2	cups whipping cream
1	cup semi-sweet chocolate morsels	½	cup light brown sugar, packed
½	cup English walnuts, chopped coarsely and toasted lightly	2	tablespoons instant coffee Nuts Chocolate shavings

- Mix brownie or cake recipe and add morsels and nuts.
- Pour into 2 (9-inch) greased round pans and bake as directed, cool.
- Whip cream until it begins to thicken, gradually add sugar and coffee until spreading consistency.
- Spread between layers and over top and sides.
- Sprinkle top with nuts and/or chocolate shavings.
- Chill overnight.

Yield: 8 servings

Piña Colada Cake

1	box yellow cake mix	1	(8-ounce) carton whipped topping
1	(12-ounce) can Piña Colada mix		
1	can condensed milk	1	(9-ounce) package frozen coconut, thawed
3	ounces pineapple juice		
1	(5-ounce) can crushed pineapple		

- Generously grease and flour 9 x 13-inch pan.
- Mix cake according to directions on box and bake at 350° for 35 to 40 minutes.
- Mix together Piña Colada mix, milk and pineapple juice.
- Pour over warm cake and set aside to cool.
- Spread crushed pineapple over cake.
- Spread whipped topping over pineapple. Sprinkle with coconut.
- Prepare the day before serving and refrigerate, covered.

Yield: 16 to 18 servings

Pineapple or Tropical Fruit Cake Mix may be used in place of yellow cake mix.

Cake Tropicale

Batter

4	eggs, beaten
1	(18½-ounce) box orange or lemon cake mix
½	cup cooking oil
1	(11-ounce) can Mandarin oranges, reserve liquid
1	teaspoon real orange flavor or Cointreau

Icing

1	(5¼-ounce) package instant pudding, vanilla or lemon
1	(20-ounce) can crushed pineapple in own juice, undrained
1	(12-ounce) whipped topping
1	(6-ounce) package frozen coconut

- Grease and flour tube pan.
- Beat eggs and add cake mix.
- Add oil, juice from can of oranges and flavoring.
- Beat together, then add oranges and beat to break-up.
- Pour in tube pan and bake 25 to 30 minutes until springs back when touched.
- Let cool on wire rack for 10 minutes, then remove from pan, cool completely. Can be wrapped and frozen at this point.
- To ice, put on plate upside down and cut through to make 3 layers.
- Mix pudding, pineapple with juice, whipped topping and coconut.
- Let rest in refrigerator for 10 minutes (more if time allows).
- Put between layers and cover cake with mixture.
- Refrigerate cake.

Yield: 12 to 15 servings

Swedish Nut Cake

Cake

2	eggs	1	teaspoon vanilla
2	cups flour	⅔	cup chopped walnuts
2	cups sugar	1	(20-ounce) can crushed
1½	teaspoons soda		pineapple, undrained

Icing

1	stick margarine, softened	1	pound powdered sugar
1	(8-ounce) package cream cheese	⅔	cup walnuts
1	teaspoon vanilla		

- Grease and flour 9 x 13-inch pan.
- Beat eggs slightly.
- Add remaining cake ingredients, beating by hand.
- Bake at 350° for 35 to 40 minutes.
- To make icing, cream margarine and cream cheese.
- Add remaining ingredients, mix well.
- Spread icing on cake when cool.

Yield: 12 servings

This cake is moist and rich.

Date Nut Cake

1	cup chopped dates
1	cup boiling water
1	teaspoon baking soda
1	cup sugar
¼	cup butter, softened
1	egg, beaten

1	teaspoon salt
1½	cups flour, sifted
½	cup chopped nuts
10	tablespoons brown sugar
10	tablespoons whipping cream
4	tablespoons butter

- Soak dates in water and baking soda, set aside.
- Cream sugar and butter; add egg, salt and flour and mix.
- Add nuts and stir to blend, add undrained dates.
- Grease 9 x 9-inch baking pan and bake at 350° for 35 minutes.
- Combine brown sugar, cream and butter in a saucepan; boil for 3 minutes, spread on hot cake.

Yield: 10 servings

Johnny Cake

2½	cups raisins
2	cups sugar
2	tablespoons vegetable oil
2	teaspoons cinnamon
1	teaspoon cloves

2	cups water
1	teaspoon baking soda
1	cup warm water
3	cups self-rising flour

- Put first 6 ingredients into a 3-quart saucepan.
- Bring to a boil, then reduce heat and cook until sugar is dissolved and raisins are soft, about 10 minutes.
- Put baking soda into cup of water and add to raisin-sugar mixture.
- Let mixture cool completely (this is a must).
- Add flour to cooled mixture.
- Pour into greased and floured 9 x 13-inch pan.
- Bake at 350° for 45 minutes on middle oven rack.

Yield: 10 to 15 servings

Oatmeal Cake

1 cup quick cooking oats	1½ cups plain flour
1½ cups boiling water	1 teaspoon nutmeg
1 stick margarine or butter, softened	1 teaspoon salt
	1 teaspoon cinnamon
1 cup sugar	1 teaspoon allspice
1½ cups dark brown sugar	1 teaspoon soda
2 eggs	

- Pour water over oats, stir and let stand 20 minutes.
- Cream margarine, sugars and eggs well.
- Sift together flour, salt, spices and soda.
- Add oats and dry ingredients to creamed mixture and beat well.
- Bake in a greased 9 x 13-inch pan at 350° for 25 minutes or until it springs back when touched.

Yield: 15 servings

Miss Ida's Chocolate Cherry Cola Cake

1 (10-ounce) jar maraschino cherries	Oil and eggs per cake mix package
1 box Devil's Food cake mix Cola (Coke or Pepsi)	Your favorite chocolate frosting

- Drain cherries, reserving juice.
- Set aside 8 whole cherries for decorating top of cake.
- Coarsely chop the remaining cherries.
- Prepare cake according to package directions omitting water; use the reserved cherry juice and enough cola to equal the water.
- Bake in 2 greased and floured 9-inch pans.
- Frost with your favorite chocolate frosting.
- Place the 8 cherries around the cake top.

Yield: 14 to 16 servings

Chocolate Fudge Sheet Cake

Cake

1 stick butter, softened	1 cup self-rising flour
1 cup sugar	1 (16-ounce) can chocolate syrup
4 eggs	1 teaspoon vanilla

- Cream butter and sugar.
- Add eggs, 1 at a time, beating after each.
- Add flour, syrup and vanilla and beat.
- Spray a 9 x 13-inch pan with cooking spray and add batter.
- Bake at 350° for 25 minutes.

Icing

1 stick butter	½ cup chocolate chips
⅓ cup evaporated milk	½ cup chopped nuts (optional)
1 cup sugar	

- Combine butter, milk and sugar in a heavy saucepan and bring to a slow boil.
- Cook 2 minutes, remove from heat and add chocolate chips and nuts.
- Beat 2 minutes and spread on cake.

Yield: 12 to 14 servings

Banana Cake

1	cup sugar	1	cup mashed bananas
½	cup butter, softened	½	cup pecans
2	eggs	½	stick butter, softened
1¾	cups flour	1	(8-ounce) package cream cheese
1	teaspoon soda	1	pound powdered sugar
1	teaspoon baking powder	½	teaspoon vanilla
¾	teaspoon salt	½	teaspoon banana flavoring
½	cup buttermilk		

- Beat sugar, butter and eggs until creamy.
- Mix flour, soda, baking powder and salt together.
- Alternate mixing dry ingredients with buttermilk into sugar mixture.
- Add banana and pecans.
- Grease and flour 2 (9-inch) cake pans and pour in the batter.
- Bake at 325° for 25 minutes, cool completely.
- Beat butter and cream cheese together.
- Add sugar, vanilla and banana flavoring.
- Spread between layers and on top of cake.

Yield: 8 to 12 servings

Carrot Cake

Cake

2 cups sugar	1½ cups cooking oil
2 cups plain flour	4 eggs
2 teaspoons cinnamon	3 cups grated carrots
2 teaspoons baking soda	1 cup chopped nuts
1 teaspoon salt	

Frosting

1 (8-ounce) package cream cheese, softened	1 teaspoon vanilla
	1 box powdered sugar
1 stick margarine, softened	1 cup nuts

- Grease and flour 2 (9-inch) or 3 (8-inch) cake pans.
- Mix all dry cake ingredients.
- Add oil and eggs.
- Add carrots and nuts, then mix well.
- Pour into pans and bake 25 to 30 minutes at 350°.
- Mix all frosting ingredients well and spread between layers and top of cake.

Yield: 12 to 14 servings

Pumpkin Cake Roll

3	eggs	½	teaspoon nutmeg
1	cup sugar	½	teaspoon salt
⅔	cup canned pumpkin	1	cup chopped pecans
1	teaspoon lemon juice	1	cup powdered sugar plus extra
¾	cup all-purpose flour		for dusting cake
1	teaspoon baking powder	2	(3-ounce) packages cream cheese
2	teaspoons cinnamon	4	tablespoons butter, softened
1	teaspoon ginger	½	teaspoon vanilla

- Beat eggs for 4 to 5 minutes.
- Gradually beat in sugar.
- Stir in pumpkin and lemon juice.
- Stir together dry ingredients and fold into pumpkin mixture.
- Spread into 15 x 10 x 1-inch pan lined with wax paper. Top with nuts.
- Bake at 375° for 10 minutes.
- Turn out on dish towel sprinkled with powdered sugar.
- Roll towel and cake, starting with narrow end, and cool completely.
- Prepare filling by beating sugar, cream cheese, butter and vanilla together until smooth.
- Roll out cake and spread with filling, remove from towel and reroll.
- Place on plate with seam side down.
- Chill 2 hours.

Yield: 10 to 12 servings

Maggie Windley's Lemon Jelly Filling

1 cup sugar	½ cup butter
3 tablespoons cornstarch	Juice of 2 lemons
Rind of 2 lemons	4 egg yolks
½ cup water	

- Mix sugar and cornstarch.
- Add lemon rind and water.
- Cook over low heat until thick.
- Add butter, lemon juice and egg yolks.
- Cook 3 to 4 minutes.
- Spread on cake immediately.

Yield: filling for a 2-layer cake

Blonde Brownies

1 cup butter	2 teaspoons baking powder
1 (16-ounce) box light brown sugar	1 teaspoon vanilla
2 eggs, beaten	Pinch salt
2 cups all-purpose flour	1 cup chopped pecans

- Preheat oven to 350°.
- Melt butter in heavy saucepan, add sugar.
- Stir in eggs, flour and baking powder.
- Add vanilla, salt and chopped pecans, mix well.
- Bake in greased 9 x 13-inch pan for 25 to 30 minutes.

Yield: 3 to 4 dozen

Ann Street Decadent Brownies

Brownies

1	stick butter or margarine, melted	2	cups sugar
½	cup Mazola oil	1	teaspoon soda
6	tablespoons cocoa	1	teaspoon cinnamon
1	cup water	2	eggs
2	cups flour	½	cup buttermilk

Frosting

5	tablespoons cocoa	1	teaspoon vanilla
6	tablespoons water	1	box powdered sugar
1	stick butter or margarine, softened	1	cup chopped nuts (optional)

- Preheat oven to 350°.
- Mix butter and oil; add cocoa and water.
- Mix dry ingredients and add to butter mixture, will be thick.
- Stir until blended, add eggs and buttermilk and stir until smooth.
- Pour into ungreased 9 x 13-inch pan and bake for 30 minutes.
- Last 5 minutes of baking, mix frosting ingredients together and spread on hot brownies, sprinkle with nuts.

Yield: 32 to 40 small squares

Brownie Cake Bars

Brownies

½ cup butter or margarine, softened	1 cup all-purpose flour, sifted
1 cup sugar	½ teaspoon baking powder
4 eggs	1 (1-pound) can chocolate syrup

Frosting

2 cups powdered sugar	½ teaspoon vanilla
4 tablespoons cocoa	3-4 tablespoons milk
4 tablespoons butter, softened	

- Preheat oven to 350°.
- Cream together butter and sugar until light and fluffy.
- Blend in eggs, 1 at a time, beating well after each.
- Sift together flour and baking powder.
- Gradually add dry ingredients to creamed mixture, mix well.
- Blend in chocolate syrup.
- Pour into greased and floured 9-inch square pan.
- Bake for 35 minutes. Cool in pan on rack.
- Combine all frosting ingredients adding enough milk to make a spreading consistency.
- Spread frosting over brownies.

Yield: 12 bars

Matt's Lemon Bars

2 cups all-purpose flour	¼ cup lemon juice
½ cup powdered sugar	2 teaspoons lemon zest (optional)
1 cup butter or margarine	⅓ cup all-purpose flour
4 eggs	1 teaspoon baking powder
2 cups sugar	Powdered sugar

- Combine flour and powdered sugar.
- Cut in butter until mixture is crumbly.
- Press mixture into a greased 9 x 13-inch baking pan.
- Bake at 325° to 350° for 15 minutes.
- Beat eggs until foamy, add sugar, lemon juice, lemon zest, flour and baking powder.
- Mix thoroughly and spread over baked crust.
- Bake at 350° for 25 to 30 minutes.
- Sprinkle with powdered sugar and cool.

Yield: 2 to 4 dozen squares

Coconut Meringue Cookies

3 egg whites, room temperature	1 teaspoon vanilla
⅛ teaspoon salt	1¼ cups shredded coconut
1 cup sugar, sifted	

- Preheat oven to 300°.
- Beat egg whites and salt until stiff.
- Add sugar very slowly, beating constantly.
- Add vanilla. Fold in coconut.
- Drop by teaspoons onto a greased and well-floured cookie sheet.
- Bake for approximately 30 minutes.

Yield: 4 dozen

Cheesecake Squares

¾	cup butter, softened	4	eggs
¾	cup brown sugar	½	tablespoon fresh lemon juice
¾	cup finely chopped pecans	½	tablespoon vanilla
2½	cups plain flour	2	cups sour cream
2	(8-ounce) packages cream cheese	4	tablespoons sugar
		1	teaspoon vanilla
1	cup sugar	¾	cup powdered sugar

- Mix butter, brown sugar, pecans and flour.
- Press on bottom and 2-inches up the sides of an 11 x 15-inch cake pan.
- Bake at 350° for 12 minutes.
- Beat cream cheese, sugar, eggs, lemon juice and vanilla together. Spread on top of baked crust.
- Bake at 350° for 10 minutes or until set.
- Mix sour cream, sugar and vanilla by hand. Spread on top of baked filling.
- Bake 10 minutes at 350°.
- Cool slightly. Sift powdered sugar over top. Refrigerate.
- Cut into squares.

Yield: 24 to 36 squares

Famous Chocolate Cookies

1	cup butter or margarine, softened	½	teaspoon salt
1	cup sugar	1	teaspoon baking powder
1	cup brown sugar	1	teaspoon soda
2	eggs	12	ounces chocolate chips
1	teaspoon vanilla	1	(4-ounce) chocolate bar, grated
2	cups all-purpose flour	1½	cups chopped nuts
2½	cups oatmeal, blend to a fine powder		

- Preheat oven to 375°.
- Cream butter and both sugars. Add eggs and vanilla.
- Mix flour, oatmeal, salt, baking powder and soda in separate bowl and add to above.
- Add chocolate chips, chocolate bar and nuts and blend well.
- Roll into balls and place 2-inches apart on cookie sheet.
- Bake for 10 minutes at 375°.

Yield: 5 dozen

"Delamar Inn"
Scottish Shortbread

3	ounces butter, softened	3	ounces all-purpose flour
1½	ounces sugar	1	ounce cornstarch

- Cream butter and sugar.
- Work in both flour and cornstarch. Knead very well - use warm hands - should be almost pastry consistency.
- Press into ungreased 2 x 8-inch round cake tin or roll to ½-inch and cut with cookie cutters.
- Bake at 300° to 325° for 40 minutes for cake or 20 minutes for cookies.
- Cool in tin. Cookies will not be brown.

Yield: 8 servings

Orange Clouds

1	cup butter, softened	2	teaspoons orange extract
⅔	cup light brown sugar, firmly packed	2¼	cups all-purpose flour
½	cup sugar	¾	teaspoon baking soda
1	large egg	½	teaspoon salt
2	tablespoons grated orange rind	2	cups white chocolate morsels

- Beat first 3 ingredients at medium speed until creamy.
- Add egg, orange rind and orange extract, beating until blended.
- Combine flour, baking soda and salt in separate bowl.
- Gradually add flour mixture to sugar mixture, beating just until blended.
- Stir in white chocolate morsels.
- Drop dough by rounded tablespoons onto ungreased cookie sheet.
- Bake at 350° for 10 to 12 minutes or until lightly browned.

Yield: 3½ dozen

Miss Georgia's Sand Tarts

½	pound butter, softened	1	teaspoon vanilla extract
4	teaspoons powdered sugar	2	cups almonds or pecans, chopped fine
¼	teaspoon salt		
2	cups plain flour		

- Combine all ingredients and roll into a log.
- Refrigerate 2½ hours.
- Slice and shape into crescents.
- Bake at 300° for 25 minutes.

Yield: 4 to 5 dozen

May be dusted with powdered sugar while warm.

Strawberry Pastries

1	sheet frozen puff pastry	1	box French vanilla pudding
1	cup milk	2	pints fresh strawberries
1	cup vanilla yogurt	3	tablespoons powdered sugar

• Remove frozen pastry and thaw at room temperature for at least 20 minutes.

• Preheat oven to 400°.

• On a work surface, gently unfold pastry, cut into 4 strips. Cut each strip crosswise into 3 pieces.

• Bake on ungreased baking sheet until puffed and golden, approximately 12 to 15 minutes.

• Place on wire rack to cool.

• Mix milk, yogurt and pudding mix until well blended.

• Hull and slice strawberries.

• Place bottom halves of pastries on serving plate.

• Spoon about 3 tablespoons of pudding onto bottom. Spoon berries over pudding.

• Cover with pastry tops.

• Sift powdered sugar over tops and serve.

Yield: 16 servings

Strawberries Marinated in Grand Marnier

2   quarts ripe strawberries   ½   cup Grand Marnier
1   cup light brown sugar

- Wash strawberries and dry them on paper towels.
- Hull berries and place in glass bowl.
- Approximately 1 hour before serving, toss strawberries gently with the brown sugar and Grand Marnier.

Yield: 8 servings

1 cup Nutra Sweet can be substituted for sugar.

Cherry Delight

2   cups white flour   2   cups 10x powdered sugar
½   cup brown sugar   2   packages Dream Whip,
1   cup butter, melted   prepared according to
½   cup finely chopped nuts   directions
2   (8-ounce) packages cream   2   (20-ounce) cans cherry pie
     cheese, softened   filling

- Beat first 4 ingredients together to make a crust.
- Pat evenly in a 9 x 13-inch baking pan.
- Bake at 350° for 15 to 20 minutes until brown and crispy.
- Remove from pan and crumble crust, put ½ back into pan and set remaining aside.
- Make a cream mixture by combining cream cheese, powdered sugar and Dream Whip.
- Spread this over crumbs, top with remaining crumbs, then pie filling.
- Chill at least 3 hours, but best prepared a day ahead.

Yield: 12 servings

Refrigerator Ambrosia

1 cup crushed pineapple, drained	1 cup chopped pecans
1½ cups sour cream	2 (11-ounce) cans Mandarin
1 cup flaked coconut	oranges, drained
1½ cups miniature marshmallows	2 cups seedless grapes, sliced

• Mix all ingredients.

• Chill for at least 8 hours before serving.

Yield: 10 to 12 servings

May be a salad or dessert.

Fresh Peach Cobbler Supreme

8 cups sliced fresh peaches	1 teaspoon almond extract
2 cups sugar	⅓ cup butter or margarine, melted
3 tablespoons all-purpose flour	Pastry for double crust pie or
½ teaspoon ground nutmeg	2 prepared crusts

• In a saucepan, combine peaches, sugar, flour and nutmeg; set aside until syrup forms.

• Bring peach mixture to a boil, reduce heat to low and cook 10 minutes or until tender.

• Remove from heat and blend in almond extract and butter.

• Roll out half of pastry dough to ⅛-inch thickness on a lightly floured board, cut to fit a 2-quart shallow casserole dish.

• Spoon half of peaches into a lightly buttered 2-quart casserole dish and top with pastry.

• Bake at 475° for 12 minutes or until golden brown.

• Spoon remaining peaches over baked pastry.

• Roll out remaining pastry and cut into ½-inch wide strips and arrange in a lattice design over peaches.

• Return to the oven for 10 to 15 minutes or until lightly browned.

Yield: 8 to 10 servings

Eva's Blueberry Crunch

Crust
1½ cups all-purpose flour

1½ sticks margarine, softened

1½ cups nuts, chopped

Cream Mixture
½ cup sugar

1 (8-ounce) package cream cheese, softened

1 (12-ounce) container whipped topping

Topping
2 tablespoons flour or 3 tablespoons cornstarch

1 cup sugar

1 pint fresh blueberries

¼ cup water

- Mix crust ingredients and pat in a 9 x 13-inch baking pan.
- Bake at 350° for 20 minutes, then cool.
- Blend ½ cup sugar and cream cheese, then fold in whipped topping.
- Spread on cooled crust.
- Fold flour into sugar, then add blueberries and water.
- Cook on medium heat on stovetop until sugar has melted and mixture begins to candy slightly.
- Cool and spread on top of cream cheese mixture.
- Refrigerate.

Yield: 12 servings

Easy Pear Bake

⅓ cup brown sugar	⅓ cup chopped nuts, toasted
¼ cup plain flour	Salt to taste
1 teaspoon cinnamon	4 large or 6 small pears, washed,
3 tablespoons butter, softened	cored and sliced thinly

- Preheat oven to 350°.
- Mix all ingredients, except pears, until mixture is in crumb stage.
- Place sliced pears in a greased 9 x 9-inch baking pan.
- Spread topping over pears and bake until pears are tender, approximately 15 minutes.
- Serve warm with ice cream or whipped cream.

Yield: 4 to 6 servings

Apple Enchiladas

1 (21-ounce) can apple pie-fruit filling	⅓ cup butter
	½ cup sugar
8-10(6 to 8-inch) flour tortillas	½ cup firmly packed brown sugar
1 teaspoon cinnamon	½ cup water

- Spoon fruit filling evenly down the center of each tortilla.
- Sprinkle each evenly with cinnamon.
- Roll up and place seam side down in a lightly greased 9 x 13-inch baking dish; may need to secure with toothpicks.
- Bring butter, sugars and water to a boil and boil for 3 minutes.
- Pour over enchiladas and let stand at least 30 minutes.
- Bake at 350° for 20 minutes.
- Serve warm topped with vanilla ice cream.

Yield: 8 to 10 servings

Sister-in-Law's Frozen Chocolate Dessert

1   (23.6-ounce) box fudge brownie
    mix
½   gallon softened vanilla ice cream
2   cups sifted powdered sugar
⅔   cup semi-sweet chocolate
    morsels

1½ cups evaporated milk
½   cup butter or margarine
1   teaspoon vanilla
1½ cups chopped nuts

- Prepare brownie mix as directed. Bake in a 9 x 13-inch pan and then cool.
- Spread ice cream on brownies and place in freezer.
- Combine sugar, chocolate morsels, milk and butter in a saucepan.
- Bring to a boil, stirring constantly.
- Reduce heat to low and cook for 8 minutes, stirring occasionally.
- Remove from heat, add vanilla and nuts.
- Cool and then pour over ice cream and brownie.
- Keep in freezer, removing about 10 minutes before cutting to serve.

Yield: 10 to 12 servings

Flan-tastic Low Fat Dessert

2   packages Jello Flan with
    caramel sauce
½   cup brewed coffee

3½ cups low fat milk
½   cup whipped topping
    Grated chocolate

- Pour packets of caramel sauce evenly in 8 (4-ounce) custard cups.
- Pour milk and coffee into saucepan.
- Add flan mix from both boxes and cook on medium heat, stirring constantly, until mixture comes to a boil.
- Pour liquid carefully over sauce in cups.
- Refrigerate at least 2 hours.
- Just before serving, unmold and top with whipped topping and grated chocolate.

Yield: 8 servings

Scrumptious Chocolate Dessert

1 box brownie mix	1 (8-ounce) carton whipped
1½ tablespoons brown sugar	topping
1 teaspoon vanilla	Chocolate curls
½ cup chocolate chips	1 cup pecan pieces, toasted
1 large chocolate instant pudding	

- Prepare brownies as directed, but increase oil to ½ cup.
- Add sugar, vanilla and chocolate chips and mix well.
- Pour into 9 x 13-inch greased pan and cook as directed.
- Cool completely.
- Prepare pudding as directed and spread over brownies. Refrigerate 1 hour.
- Cover with whipped topping, add chocolate curls and nuts to decorate. Keep refrigerated.

Yield: 15 servings

Served at ECW Fall Bazaar luncheon; also great for covered dish dinners.

Toffee

1 pound butter	12 ounces milk chocolate, grated
2 cups sugar	⅔ cup walnuts, chopped fine
1 cup blanched and chopped almonds	

- Melt butter in heavy saucepan over low heat.
- Add sugar and almonds.
- Increase heat to medium high and stir constantly until mixture turns to toffee (300° on a candy thermometer).
- Pour into 11 x 16-inch ungreased jellyroll pan or cookie sheet with sides; spread to edges.
- Top with grated chocolate and sprinkle with nuts.
- Allow cooling and setting overnight, breaking into chunks.

Yield: 36 to 48 pieces

Bread Pudding

3	large eggs, lightly beaten	½	cup sugar
1½	cups sugar	3	tablespoons brown sugar
2	tablespoons light brown sugar	1	tablespoon flour
½	teaspoon ground nutmeg		Dash nutmeg
¼	cup butter, melted	1	large egg
2¾	cups whipping cream	2	tablespoons butter
4	cups cubed French bread	1¼	cups whipped cream
¾	cup golden raisins	1	tablespoon vanilla

- Combine first 4 ingredients, stir in butter and cream.
- Gently stir in bread and raisins, pour into a 2-quart lightly greased baking dish.
- Bake at 375° for 50 to 55 minutes, cover lightly with foil after 30 minutes.
- Remove from oven and let stand 30 minutes.
- For sauce, whisk sugars, flour, nutmeg, egg, butter and cream over medium heat.
- Whisk constantly about 10 minutes or until thickened; stir in vanilla.
- Serve pudding with sauce poured over it.

Yield: 12 to 15 servings

Unbaked pudding can be prepared and refrigerated a day ahead. Bring to room temperature for 30 minutes before baking.

Bread Pudding with Bourbon Sauce

8	cups dry bread crumbs (biscuits work well)	1	cup raisins
1	quart whole milk	½-1	cup crushed pineapple, drained
1	stick butter, softened	1	stick butter or margarine
1½	cups sugar	1	cup powdered sugar, sifted
4	eggs	1	egg, beaten
1	tablespoon vanilla	¼-½	cup bourbon, to taste

- Tear or cube bread in a large bowl and add milk to cover. Soak 1 hour.
- In another bowl, mix butter and sugar.
- Add eggs and mix well.
- Add vanilla and then bread mixture and mix well.
- Stir in raisins and pineapple.
- Pour into greased 9 x 13-inch baking dish.
- Bake at 350° for 45 to 60 minutes or until firm.
- When ready to serve, make sauce of butter, sugar and egg.
- Melt butter in saucepan; add sugar and stir until smooth.
- Stir in beaten egg and cook over low to medium heat until thoroughly blended.
- Remove from heat and blend in bourbon.
- Serve warm over pudding.

Yield: 12 to 15 servings

Fool-Proof Fudge

3   (6-ounce) bags chocolate   Dash salt
     morsels (semi-sweet or milk   1½   teaspoons vanilla
     chocolate)   ½   cup chopped nuts (optional)
1   can condensed sweetened milk

- In a heavy saucepan over low heat, melt chocolate pieces in milk.
- Stir until smooth.
- Remove from heat.
- Add dash of salt and vanilla. Add nuts if desired.
- Stir and pour into wax paper-lined 7 x 11-inch pan.
- Chill until firm, turn onto cutting board and cut into squares.
- Store loosely covered at room temperature.

Yield: 24 to 32 squares

Microwave Dixie Peanut Brittle

1½   cups raw shelled peanuts with   ⅛   teaspoon salt
      skins on   1   teaspoon butter
1   cup sugar   1   teaspoon vanilla
½   cup light corn syrup   1   teaspoon baking soda

- In a 1½-quart casserole dish, stir together peanuts, sugar, syrup and salt.
- Cook 8 minutes on high in microwave oven, stirring well after 4 minutes of cooking.
- Stir in butter and vanilla. Microwave 2 more minutes on high.
- Add baking soda and quickly stir until light and foamy.
- Immediately pour into lightly greased baking sheet, spread out very thin.
- When cool break into small pieces, store in airtight container.

Yield: 1 pound

Microwave Fudge

1	pound sifted powdered sugar	¼	cup milk
½	stick butter	½	teaspoon vanilla
¼	cup cocoa	½	cup chopped nuts

- Place sugar, butter, cocoa and milk in a glass mixing bowl, do not mix.
- Microwave on high for 4 minutes.
- Mix well, stir in vanilla and nuts.
- Pour in lightly buttered 8 x 8-inch dish.
- Refrigerate until cooled, cut into desired squares.

Yield: 16 to 24 squares

Chocolate Whiskey Truffles

8	ounces semi-sweet chocolate, chopped	3	tablespoons Jack Daniels Whiskey
½	cup unsalted butter	½	cup unsweetened cocoa powder
⅔	cup finely crushed gingersnap cookies	½	cup powdered sugar

- Melt chocolate and butter in heavy medium saucepan over low heat, stirring until smooth.
- Mix in crushed cookies and whiskey.
- Line cookie sheet with foil.
- Drop truffle mixture by tablespoons onto foil, spacing apart. Freeze 15 minutes.
- Roll each between palms of hands into smooth round.
- Sift cocoa powder and sugar into shallow dish. Roll each truffle in cocoa mixture.

Yield: 20 to 24

Can be prepared 1 week ahead. Cover and refrigerate in airtight container. Let stand 15 minutes at room temperature before serving.

Menus for Special Occasions

before restoration

1796 court house

after restoration

The Carteret County
Courthouse of 1796 - Pen and Ink

Mamré Marsh Wilson

Ms. Wilson is a Beaufort resident and a member and on staff
at St. Paul's. Although she studied art for one year while in
college, she did not pursue it as a career. However, she continued
to draw, illustrate, and use her creativity in her work while
developing her pen and ink artistry. She continues to design
and draw, particularly pen and ink sketches, but
she also enjoys writing.

Menus for Special Occasions

ᐧ Lenten Church Suppers ᐧ

Homemade Vegetable Soup, page 76
Festive Black Bean Chili, page 72
Puttanesca Sauce for Pasta, page 164
Double Deluxe Cornbread, page 48
Apple Carrot Muffins, page 39
Eva's Blueberry Crunch, page 227
Easy Pear Bake, page 228

ᐧ ECW Bazaar Luncheon ᐧ

Southern Chicken Salad, page 102 or
Chicken and Broccoli Casserole, page 131
Sweet Potato Soufflé, page 121
Green Beans
Cranberry Salad, page 82
Anne's Parmesan Biscuits, page 46
Extra Elegant Apple Pie, page 184 or
Scrumptious Chocolate Dessert, page 230

ᐧ Sunday School Class Oyster Roast ᐧ

Roasted Oysters and Clams
Fried Menhaden Roe, page 182
Assorted Sandwiches
Hot Beef Dip, page 22
Artichoke-Filled French Bread, page 15
Squash Cornbread, page 49
Apple Cake Squares, page 205
Caramel Coconut Pie, page 193

༝ Altar Guild Tea ༺

Orange Tea Sandwiches, page 35
Veggie Bars, page 11
Front Street Shrimp Spread, page 5
Toasted Parmesan Canapés, page 20
Hot Crab Dip, page 22
Marinated Cheese, page 18
Angel Biscuits with Smithfield Ham, page 46
Matt's Lemon Bars, page 220
Miss Georgia's Sand tarts, page 223
Brownie Cake Bars, page 219
Instant Party Punch, page 29 or Hot Cranberry Tea, page 34

༝ Old Homes Tour ECW Lunch Sale ༺

Assorted Toppings on Dot's Bread, page 41
Eight Veggie Sandwich Spread, page 51 or
Pimento Cheese Sandwich Spreads, page 52 or Egg Salad Sandwich
Hot Dogs with Chili
Potato Chips or Summer Potato Salad, page 100
Blonde Brownies, page 217 or Piña Colada Cake, page 208
Iced Tea

༝ Sunday Picnic at the Knob ༺

Grilled Burgers, Hot Dogs and Smoked Sausage
Barbecued Chicken and Ribs
Captain Christian's Gazpacho, page 80
Five Bean Salad, page 99
Blue Cheese Potato Salad, page 100
Shrimp and Seashells, page 103
Deviled Eggs
Fresh Peach Cobbler Supreme, page 226
Famous Chocolate Cookies, page 222

↶ New Year's Day Brunch ↷

Anne's Bloody Mary Mix, page 30
Jean T's Cheese Circles, page 16
Shrimp Sea Island, page 28
Easy Breakfast Casserole, page 54
Oakwood Acres Collard Casserole, page 110
Black-Eye Pea Salad, page 98
Southern Grits Casserole, page 56
Baked Fruit Casserole, page 129
Pumpkin Cake Roll, page 216
Fran's Monkey Bread, page 39
Streusel-Filled Coffee Cake, page 44

↶ St. Paul's Covered Dish Dinner Sampler ↷

Saucy Meat Loaf, page 157
Hilton Head Casserole, page 158
Chicken and Beef Casserole, page 136
Different Baked Ham, page 145
Broccoli Casserole, page 108
Scalloped Tomatoes, page 125
Roasted Vegetables with Herbs and Garlic, page 128
Congealed Fruit Salad, page 85
Miss Matt's Lemon Meringue Pie, page 183
Chocolate Fudge Sheet Cake, page 213

↶ House Blessing Reception or Buffet ↷

Manhattan Meatballs, page 26
Marinated Beef Tenderloin, page 152 with Yeast Rolls, page 41
Net House Shrimp Quiche, page 181
Chicken Salad Hugo, page 102
Mushroom Pâté, page 12
Vegetable Trio, page 107 or Spinach Squares, page 122
Fresh Fruit Salad, page 88
Almond Pound Cake with Caramel Icing, page 195
Beaufort Grocery Co. Lemon Cheesecake, page 206
Strawberry Pastries, page 224
Supper Club Whiskey Sour Punch, page 31 or
Joyce's Special Champagne Punch, page 30

Committees and Contributors

Cookbook Steering Committee

Suzanne Bullard   Anne Eastman   Judy Mercer
Bitsy Dudley   Mary Duane Hale   Ginny Poindexter

Cookbook Art Committee

Rosemary Green, Photographer   Ginny Poindexter
Ann Hauman, Graphics   Lynda Steed
Cydney Dee Smith, Waterfront Junction Framers

ECW Officers

1998-1999   **2000-2001**
Mary Duane Hale, President   Lanny Wase, President
Lanny Wase, Vice-President   Ginny Poindexter,Vice-President
Ilse Englehardt, Secretary   Ilse Englehardt, Secretary
June Smith, Treasurer   June Smith, Treasurer
Nancy Conner, Director   Mary Duane Hale, Director
Mary Lou Hill, Director   Fran Rock, Director

Art Contributors

Special thanks to Rosemary Green for photographing all the artwork and Ann Hauman for her pen and ink graphics used throughout the cookbook. We would also like to thank all the other artists whose work is seen throughout this cookbook for sharing their work with us:

Audrey Evans   Nancy L. Rogers,   Millie Voorhees
Doris King   A.S.I.D.   Jim Williams
Richard Meelheim   Lynda Fodrie Steed   Mamré Marsh Wilson
Laura Davis Piner   Lisa Stockard

Special Recipe Contributors

We would like to thank the following restaurants, bed and breakfasts, and businesses for donating their special recipes:

Beaufort Grocery Co., Beaufort, N.C.   The Net House, Beaufort, N.C.
Cousins Bed and Breakfast, Beaufort, N.C.   "On a Roll" Gourmet Deli, Morehead
Delamar Inn, Beaufort, N.C.   City, N.C.
G & R Supermarket, Smyrna, N.C.   Pecan Tree Inn, Beaufort, N.C.
Ginny Gordon's Gifts and Gadgets,   Stillwater Café, Beaufort, N.C.
  Morehead City, N.C.

Recipe Contributors

We would like to thank all the members, families, and friends of St. Paul's for donating their treasured recipes for this cookbook. We especially acknowledge all the St. Paul's Church Women who have tested and edited the recipes as well as raising all the funds to make this cookbook possible. We are truly grateful to all these individuals who have given of their time and talents:

Tina Banks	Lynn Darden	Charles Hale
Marilyn Barnes	Mary Lee Daughtry	Mary Duane Hale
Anne Blackwell	Lucy Davis	Evelyn Hassell
Jean Bloodgood	William Moore Davis	Jenny Hassinger
Kathy Bohley	Patti Dill	Ann Hauman
Carolyn Boothe	Anne Dishong	Joyce Hewett
Bert Brooks	Tammy Dodds	Mary Lou Hill
Gina Brooks	Bitsy Dudley	Terri Hines
Jerri Brooks	Donnie Dudley	Lenna Hobson
Bern Bullard	Jane Dudley	Sandra Howarth
Suzanne Bullard	Dana Dunne	Joe Johnson
Jane Bullock	T.J. Dunne	Shirley Johnson
Lois Burger	Lea Eason	Peggy Jones
Hazel Byrd	Anne Eastman	Robert Jones
Brenda Chadwick	Lynne Eastman	Brownie King
Joyce Chadwick	Betty Lou Ellis	Doris King
Emy Christian	Ilse Englehardt	Paula King
Joe Christian	Lillian Flynn	Kathy Kirkman
Beth Clawson	Margaret Fondry	Joyce Lewis
Imogene Clawson	George Frazier	Nancy Lewis
Claudia Clingman	Pat Frazier	Penny Lloyd
Kathryn Cloud	Nancy Freeman	Shelvy Lloyd
Anne Collins	Evelyn Fulcher	Bob Lloyd
Joan Coogan	Wanda Gaskill	Christy Maroules
Molly Coogan	Len Gilstrap	Barbara Martin
Nancy Connor	Tonia Glasgow	Joan Martini
Ginny Costlow	Eda Gordon	Connie Mason
Dot Covert	Kathy Grant	Jolene McCann
Gretchen Creel	May Gray	Arnette McDevett
Kelly Creelman	Rosemary Green	Sandra McDonald
Nan Cullman	Casey Griffin	

(continued on next page)

Martha McGavern
Richard McGavern
Kay Mease
Delores Meelheim
Judy Mercer
Elizabeth Mewborne
Peg Midyette
Tommy Midgett
Barbara Milhaven
Rosemary Miller
Hilda Mitchell
Nancy Moore
Sallie Poole Moore
Kaki Murphy
Jane Nelson
Kathryn Nelson
Ruth O'Bryan
Sue Oettinger
Mary Ogus
Helen O'Neal
Lavinia Owens
Merry Palazzo
Charles Park
Marnie Park
Wendy Park
Shirley Pedersen
Pam Phillips
Patricia Phillips
Julie Pittman
Pat Pitts
Charles Poindexter

Ginny Poindexter
Vonda Pollitt
Pinky Porter
Fran Potter
Pat Potter
Elizabeth Powell
Ciaren Prentice
Lauralee Prentice
Gail Quante
Mary Lou Redd
Pam Roberts
Fran Rock
Lena Rudder
Nancy Russell
Sarah Jo Safrit
Kay Salter
Madeline Schaw
Sallie Searle
Julia Sebes
Evelyn Sewell
Kathleen Moore Shank
Flo Shedd
Irene Slater
June Smith
Nancy Smith
Lynda Steed
Nancy Stephenson
Cynthia Stevens
Lisa Stockard
Matt Stockard
David Stout

Patricia Suggs
Phyllis Tally
Billy Taylor
Maxine Taylor
Gwyndolyn Towles
Nancy Ustach
John VanRavestein
Dot Waldenmaier
Lanny Wase
Jean Watkins
Sissy Weil
Sarah West
Alice Wheatly
Joyce Wheatly
Nancy Wheatly
Sandra Wheatly
Sylvia Wheatly
Park White
Patty White
Ann Williams
Kathryn Williams
Sandra Williams
Carol Willis
Ralph Willis
Verta Willis
Dorothy Wilson
Georgia Wood
Sylvia H. Woolard
Mary Louise Wooten
Marilyn Zmoda

Index

INDEX

Let Us Keep The Feast in Historic Beaufort

St. Paul's ECW
215 Ann Street
Beaufort, NC 28516

Please send me _____ copies   @ $19.95 each _____

Postage and handling   @ $ 3.50 each _____

                                               Total _____

Name _____

Address _____

City _____ State _____ Zip _____

Make check payable to: **St. Paul's ECW**

- -

Let Us Keep The Feast in Historic Beaufort

St. Paul's ECW
215 Ann Street
Beaufort, NC 28516

Please send me _____ copies   @ $19.95 each _____

Postage and handling   @ $ 3.50 each _____

                                               Total _____

Name _____

Address _____

City _____ State _____ Zip _____

Make check payable to: **St. Paul's ECW**